BREAD AND CAKES

BREAD AND CAKES

by Anne Chamberlain

LONDON
W FOULSHAM & CO LTD
New York   Toronto   Cape Town   Sydney

W Foulsham & Co Ltd
Yeovil Road, Slough, Berks, England

ISBN 0-572-00998-4

Photoset and printed in Great Britain by
Lowe & Brydone Printers Limited, Thetford, Norfolk

CONTENTS

METRICATION

It is very important to use either the imperial table for measuring ingredients *or* the metric one, and not to mix them when preparing a recipe. The metric scale is not an exact translation of the imperial one, which would be very cumbersome, but the recipes have been tested to arrive at the correct proportions. The metric result is approximately 10% less than that gained with imperial measurements.

The metric scale recommended for British use allows 25 g to 1 oz; and 25 ml to 1 fl oz, instead of the true scale of 28 g to 1 oz. This means that quantities must be 'rounded up' at certain points on the scale, or else vital amounts will be lost as total recipe quantities become larger.

Solid Measures

½ oz	15 g
1 oz	25 g
2 oz	50 g
3 oz	75 g
4 oz	100 g
5 oz	125 g
6 oz	150 g
7 oz	175 g
8 oz	225 g
9 oz	250 g
10 oz	300 g
11 oz	325 g
12 oz	350 g
13 oz	375 g
14 oz	400 g
15 oz	425 g
16 oz	450 g or 500 g
1½ lb	750 g
2 lb	1 kg

Liquid Measures

½ fl oz	15 ml
1 fl oz	25 ml
2 fl oz	50 ml
3 fl oz	75 ml
4 fl oz	100 ml
¼ pint	125 ml
⅓ pint	175 ml
½ pint	250 ml
⅔ pint	350 ml
¾ pint	375 ml
1 pint	500 ml
1¼ pints	625 ml
1½ pints	750 ml
1¾—2 pints	1 litre

When meat and vegetables and some groceries are purchased in metric measure, they will normally be in 1 lb or 2 lb measurement equivalents, and people will ask for .5 kg or 1 kg which is 500 g or 1000 g. When baking, a measurement of 450 g is in proportion with the smaller amounts of ingredients needed.

INTRODUCTION

Home-baking is one of the most satisfactory kinds of cooking. There is nothing like the scent of home-made bread, the succulence of a rich fruit cake, the delight of an airy meringue or feathery eclair, or the crispness of a fresh-from-the-oven biscuit.

There are no hidden secrets in successful bread and cake making. Anyone who can switch on an oven, weigh ingredients carefully and follow a recipe exactly will be successful. Always take time to read a recipe, and collect ingredients together before you begin. Then weigh the ingredients accurately and mix them as directed. Be sure the oven is switched on before you start mixing, and do use the correct tins. Although there is no 'magic' in baking, there is the need for scientific accuracy. Nobody will notice particularly if you vary the ingredients in a casserole, or leave out one of them, but the balance of a good baking recipe is very important, and only care will produce perfect results every time.

Chapter One

BREAD, YEAST CAKES AND BUNS

Don't be frightened of working with yeast. It is a living ingredient which loves warmth and a little sweetness. Buy fresh yeast from a baker or health food shop, or packaged dried yeast from a grocer or chemist. If you are adapting recipes, you will find that you only need half as much dried yeast as fresh yeast. Yeast needs a moist warmth to allow it to develop before being added to dry ingredients. Fresh yeast will quickly start to bubble and work, but dried yeast will take 10—20 minutes to become active and frothy, so give it time. Keep mixing bowls warm (but not hot) and see that liquid is just hand-hot.

It is important to use the correct flour for breadmaking. This is now available in all grocers under the name of 'bread flour' or 'strong plain flour'. When yeast is used with this flour, it creates a dough which will be soft and aerated when baked. A little fat added to bread dough improves texture and keeping quality; salt is essential for a good flavour.

Basically, a dough is mixed with flour and a liquid in which the yeast has been mixed. This dough has to be worked together and kneaded so that the yeast cells are thoroughly distributed through the dough. The dough is then left in a warm place to rise or 'prove' for a given time, then 'knocked back' or kneaded again and shaped. The shaped loaves or buns are again left to rise, and are finally baked in a hot oven. When yeast dough sounds hollow when tapped, it is fully cooked.

Basic White Bread

Dry Mix

	Imperial	Metric	American
Strong plain flour	3 lb	1.5 kg	12 cups
Salt	1 oz	25 g	2 tbsp

Yeast Liquid

Blend 1 oz/25 g fresh yeast in ½ pint/250 ml/1¼ cups water *or* Dissolve 1 teaspoon sugar in ½ pint/250 ml/1¼ cups warm water. Sprinkle on 1 level tablespoon dried yeast. Leave until frothy – about 10 minutes.

Additional ingredients

	Imperial	Metric	American
Lard, rubbed into dry mix	1 oz	25 g	2 tbsp
Water	1 pint	500 ml	2½ cups

Mix dry ingredients with yeast liquid and water. Work to a firm dough, adding extra flour if needed, until the dough leaves the bowl clean. Turn the dough on to a lightly floured board, knead and stretch the dough, by folding forward then pushing down and away with palm of hand. Give dough a quarter turn and repeat kneading, developing a rocking rhythm until it feels firm and elastic and no longer sticky (about 10 minutes). Shape the kneaded dough into a round ball and place in a large lightly greased polythene bag, lightly tied. Stand the dough to rise until it doubles in size, and springs back when lightly pressed with a floured finger. Rising time can be varied:

45—60 minutes in a warm place

2 hours at average room temperature

12 hours in a cold room or larder

24 hours in a refrigerator (refrigerated dough must be allowed to return to room temperature before shaping)

Turn the dough on to a lightly floured board, divide into four, flatten each piece firmly with the knuckles to knock out the air bubbles, and knead to make a firm dough. To make a tin loaf, shape each piece by either folding in three, or rolling up like a Swiss roll; tuck the ends under. The dough piece should exactly fit the tin. Place each dough piece in a greased 1 lb/45 g loaf tin, put inside a lightly greased polythene bag, and put aside until the dough rises to the tops of the tins, 1—1½ hours at room temperature, longer in a refrigerator. Remove the polythene cover.

Bake the loaves in the centre of a hot oven set at 450 °F/230 °C/Gas Mark 8 for 30—40 minutes or until the loaves shrink slightly from the sides of the tin and the crust is deep golden brown. For a crustier loaf turn the loaves out on to a baking sheet and bake for a futher 5—10 minutes. When sufficiently baked the loaves should sound hollow when tapped on the base. Cool on a wire rack.

Loaves may be brushed before baking, with water, milk, beaten egg and water or milk and a pinch of sugar or egg white. For a change, sprinkle a few poppy seeds on top.

Basic White Dough

	Imperial	Metric	American
Strong plain white flour	3 lb	1.5 kg	12 cups
Salt	1 oz	25 g	2 tbsp
Lard	1 oz	25 g	2 tbsp
Fresh yeast **or**	1 oz	25 g	1 oz
Dried yeast	½ oz	15 g	½ oz
Sugar	1 tsp	1 tsp	1 tsp
Warm water	1½ pints	750 ml	3¾ cups

Mix flour and salt and rub in fat. Prepare yeast liquid: dried yeast should be reconstituted by putting ¼ pint/125 ml/½ cup measured liquid into a small jug. Stir in the sugar and sprinkle the dried yeast on to the liquid. Leave in a warm place until frothy – about 10—15 minutes. Fresh yeast will only take a minute or two to become frothy. Add yeast liquid and remaining water to flour mixture. Mix well, then turn on to a board and knead for 10 minutes. Place dough in a greased bowl and place bowl in a large oiled polythene bag. Leave until dough has doubled in size, about an hour in a warm place. Turn dough on to a lightly floured board and knead for about 5 minutes. Divide dough into 3 and finish according to recipe.

Cheese and Celery Plait

Work 1 teaspoon mustard powder and 4 oz/100 g/ 1 cup finely grated cheese into the dough by squeezing and kneading the dough until the ingredients are thoroughly mixed in. Divide the dough into 3 and roll each piece in a long sausage. Plait the pieces together, brushing the ends with beaten egg to secure firmly. Place on a greased baking tray and place inside a large oiled polythene bag. Leave until doubled in size. Remove polythene bag. Sprinkle the plait with 1 oz/25 g/¼ cup

grated cheese and 1 teaspoon celery salt. Bake at 400 °
F/200 °C/Gas Mark 6 for 30—35 minutes.

Garlic and Herb Wheels

Work 2 crushed garlic cloves and 2 teaspoons
mixed dried herbs into the dough by squeezing and
kneading the dough until the herbs are thoroughly mixed
in. Divide dough into approximately 15. Roll each piece of
dough into a length 6 in./15 cm long. Coil the length of the
dough starting at the centre. Place on greased baking
trays. Leave for 10 minutes in a warm place covered with
an oiled polythene bag. Glaze with egg for a golden crust.
Bake at 425 °F/220 °C/Gas Mark 7 for 10—15 minutes.

Iced Tea Ring

Roll out the dough to an oblong approx. 14 × 10 in./
35 × 25 cm. Mix 4 oz/100 g/½ cup dried mixed fruit
1 oz/25 g/2 tablespoons demerara sugar and a pinch of
mixed spice. Sprinkle over the dough to within 1 in./2.5
cm of the edge. Damp the edges and seal well. Form into a
circle on a baking sheet, sealing ends together well with
water. Cover with an oiled polythene bag, stand in a warm
place and leave until doubled in size. Bake at 400 °F/200 °
C/Gas Mark 6. When cool cover with glacé icing made by
mixing 3 oz/75 g/6 tablespoons icing sugar with 2
tablespoons lemon juice. Sprinkle with flaked almonds
and glacé cherries.

Basic Wheatmeal Dough

	Imperial	Metric	American
Strong brown wheatmeal flour	3 lb	1.5 kg	12 cups
Salt	1 oz	25 g	2 tbsp
Lard	1 oz	25 g	2 tbsp
Fresh yeast **or**	1 oz	25 g	1 oz
Dried yeast	½ oz	15 g	½ oz
Sugar	1 tsp	1 tsp	1 tsp
Warm water	1½ pints	750 ml	3¾ cups

Mix flour and salt and rub in fat. Prepare yeast liquid: dried yeast should be reconstituted by putting ¼ pint/125 ml/½ cup of the measured liquid into a small jug. Stir in the sugar and sprinkle the dried yeast onto the liquid. Leave in a warm place until frothy – about 10—15 minutes. Fresh yeast will only take a minute or two to become frothy. Add yeast liquid and remaining water to flour mixture. Mix well, then turn on to a board and knead for 10 minutes. Place dough in a greased bowl, place bowl in a large oiled polythene bag. Leave dough until it has doubled in size about 1—1½ hours in a warm place. Turn dough on to a floured board and knead again. Divide dough in half. Use one half to make a crown load and divide remaining half into 3 using ⅓ for a cottage loaf and the other ⅔ for pizza bases.

Crown Loaf

Divide dough into 10 equal pieces and shape each into a round. Grease a 10 in./25 cm round cake tin and place the rolls in it with 7 around the edge and 3 in the centre. Prove for 30—35 minutes, covered with a large, oiled polythene bag. Glaze with beaten egg and milk to give a golden crust and scatter with poppy or sesame seeds. Bake at 400 °F/200 °C/Gas Mark 6 for 30—35 minutes.

Cottage Loaf

Cut off ⅓ of the dough and shape one small and one large ball. Brush a little milk on the centre of the large ball and place the smaller ball on the top. Flour the handle of a wooden spoon and push it right through both balls and then pull it out sharply. Leave for 10 minutes, in a warm place covered with an oiled polythene bag. Dust with flour before baking for a soft crust. Bake at 425 ° F/220 °C/Gas Mark 7 for 20—25 minutes.

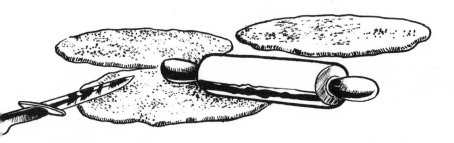

Pizza Bases

Roll out remaining 2 pieces of dough into 2 rounds, 9 in./22.5 cm in diameter. Place one on a greased baking tray (this can be cooked to eat immediately) and the other on a tray or plate to freeze for a later date. Cover both the pizza bases with topping to within ½ in./1.25 cm of the edge. Leave the one to be cooked now in a warm place for 15 minutes then bake at 425 °F/220 °C/Gas Mark 7 for 25—30 minutes.

Pizza Toppings
Tomato Sauce

	Imperial	Metric	American
Oil	1 tbsp	1 tbsp	1 tbsp
1 large onion			
Canned tomatoes	14 oz	400 g	1¾ cups
Tomato puree	1 tbsp	1 tbsp	1 tbsp
Salt and pepper			
Dried marjoram	½ tsp	½ tsp	½ tsp

Lightly fry chopped onion in oil until soft. Add remaining ingredients and simmer for 10—15 minutes until liquid has evaporated. Divide the tomato sauce mixture between the 2 pizza bases, spreading it to within ½ in./1.25 cm of the edge. Arrange either of the following on the top.

Olive and Salami

	Imperial	Metric	American
Salami	3 oz	75 g	3 oz
Black olives, halved and pitted	6	6	6
Parmesan cheese, grated	1 tbsp	1 tbsp	1 tbsp

Cheese and Sardine

	Imperial	Metric	American
Mozzarella cheese, sliced	3 oz	75 g	3 oz
Small can sardines in oil, drained, halved and boned	1	1	1

Muffins

	Imperial	Metric	American
Strong plain flour	1 lb	450 g	4 cups
Salt	1 tsp	1 tsp	1 tsp
Fresh yeast **or**	½ oz	15 g	½ oz
Dried yeast	¼ oz	8 g	¼ oz
Warm water	½ pint	250 ml	1¼ cups

Make yeast liquid with yeast and water. Add yeast liquid to flour and salt and knead until dough is smooth. Place in greased polythene bag and leave to rise for about 1 hour at room temperature. The dough is ready when it springs back if pressed with a lightly floured finger. Knead lightly again and roll out on floured board to ½ in./1.25 cm thickness. Leave to rest for 5 minutes, covered, and cut into 3½ in./9 cm rounds. Re-roll and cut until all dough is used up. Place on well-floured baking sheet and dust tops with flour or fine semolina. Place in large polythene bag and leave for 30—40 minutes at room temperature. Test with floured finger again. Cook on hot, greased girdle, frying pan or hotplate for about 6 minutes each side, until golden brown. Alternatively bake at 450 °F/230 °C/Gas Mark 8 for 10 minutes, turning after 5 minutes. To serve, pull muffins open all the way round with the fingers, leaving the two halves joined in the middle, and toast slowly on both sides. Pull apart, butter each half well, put together again and serve hot.

Wiltshire Lardy Cake

	Imperial	Metric	American
Risen white bread dough	1½ lb	750 g	1½ lb
Lard or butter	4 oz	100 g	½ cup
Caster sugar	4 oz	100 g	½ cup
Ground mixed spice (optional)	1 tsp	1 tsp	1 tsp
Sultanas (optional)	4 oz	100 g	1 cup

Turn the dough on to lightly floured board and roll firmly to ¼ in./65 mm thick strip with a rolling pin. Spread one-third of the sugar and spice and sultanas if used, and fold into three. Roll out to a strip again and repeat procedure with fat and sugar. Repeat twice more. Put the rolled dough in a baking tin, 8 x10 in./20 x 25 cm and press down firmly to fill up the corners. Criss-cross the top by lightly scoring with a very sharp knife. Place in a lightly greased polythene bag and allow to rise to double in size. Bake at 425 °F/220 °C/Gas Mark 7 for 30 minutes. Remove from the tin and spoon any syrup remaining in the tin over the surface of the cake.

Currant Loaf

	Imperial	Metric	American
Strong plain flour	1 lb	450g	4 cups
Sugar	1 oz	25 g	2 tbsp
Salt	1 tsp	1 tsp	1 tsp
Butter	1 oz	25 g	2 tbsp
Currants	4 oz	100 g	1 cup
Fresh yeast	1 oz	25 g	1 oz
Milk and water	½ pint	250 ml	1¼ cups

Cream yeast with lukewarm liquid. Mix flour, sugar and salt, rub in butter and mix in currants. Add yeast liquid and work to a firm dough, adding extra flour if needed, until the dough leaves the bowl clean. Turn the dough on to a lightly floured board and knead by stretching and folding until the dough is smooth and elastic. Divide in two, flatten each piece and roll up like a Swiss roll to fit two greased 1 lb/450 g loaf tins. Place tins in lightly greased polythene bags and leave to rise until dough doubles in size and springs back when lightly pressed with a floured finger. Remove polythene. Bake at 425 °F/220 °C Gas Mark 7 for 45 minutes. Brush tops of hot loaves with a wet brush dipped in honey. Cool on a wire tray.

Hot Cross Buns

	Imperial	Metric	American
Clear honey	3 tbsp + 1 tsp	3 tbsp + 1 tsp	3 tbsp + 1 tsp
Milk	4 fl oz	100 ml	½ cup
Fresh yeast **or**	½ oz	15 g	½ oz
Dried yeast	¼ oz	8 g	¼ oz
Strong plain flour	12 oz	350 g	3 cups
Salt	½ tsp	½ tsp	½ tsp
Ground mixed spice	1—1½ tsp	1—1½ tsp	1—1½ tsp
Ground cinnamon	½ tsp	½ tsp	½ tsp
Butter	2½ oz	65 g	5 tbsp
Egg	1	1	1
Dried fruit	3 oz	75 g	¾ cup
Shortcrust pastry for crosses			

Glaze

	Imperial	Metric	American
Milk	1 tbsp	1 tbsp	1 tbsp
Sugar	1 tbsp	1 tbsp	1 tbsp

Dissolve 1 teaspoon honey in 3 tablespoons warm milk and mix the yeast into the sweet milk. Sieve the flour, salt and spices into a bowl. Leave the yeast mixture and the flour in a warm place for 15—20 minutes until the yeast has a frothy head. Heat the remaining milk and honey with the butter to blood heat. Mix the yeast liquid, the beaten egg and the milk and honey into the flour to form a soft dough. Knead for about 5 minutes then place in a greased bowl, cover and leave in a warm place until the mixture has doubled in size. Knead the fruit into the mixture, divide into 12, shape into small rounds. Place the buns on a greased baking sheet allowing enough room for the buns to rise. Leave in a warm place for 15—20 minutes. Roll the pastry out thinly, cut into strips, dampen and place on the top of the risen buns, gently pressing them into the sides of the buns. Bake at 425 °F/ 220 °C/Gas Mark 7 for about 15 minutes until golden brown. When the buns are tapped on the bottom they should sound hollow. Cool on a wire rack. Make the glaze by gently heating the milk and sugar together until the sugar has dissolved, brush over the buns as soon as they are removed from the oven.

Chelsea Buns

	Imperial	Metric	American
Plain flour	12 oz	350 g	3 cups
Butter	3 oz	75 g	1/3 cup
Fresh yeast	1/2 oz	15 g	1/2 oz
Sugar	1 tsp	1 tsp	1 tsp
Milk	8 fl oz	200 ml	1 cup
Sugar	2 oz	50 g	1/4 cup
Currants	2 oz	50 g	1/3 cup

Put the flour into a warm bowl and add two-thirds butter. Cream the yeast with the sugar and add warm milk. Stir into the flour and knead thoroughly. Cover and leave for 45 minutes until the dough has doubled in size. Knead into a rectangle. Melt the remaining butter and brush over the dough. Sprinkle with sugar and currants and roll up firmly like a Swiss roll. Cut across into 1½ ins/3.75 cm thick slices. Put these pieces cut side up on a greased baking tray, fairly close together but leaving room to swell. Leave in a warm place for 10 minutes and brush with a little beaten egg. Bake at 450 °F/230 °C/Gas Mark 8 for 15 minutes. Melt 1 tablespoon sugar with 2 tablespoons milk and brush this over the buns as soon as they come from the oven, then sprinkle with a little sugar.

Sultana Malt Bread

	Imperial	Metric	American
Strong plain flour	1 lb	450 g	4 cups
Salt	1 tsp	1 tsp	1 tsp
Sultanas	8 oz	225 g	2 cups
Fresh yeast	1 oz	25 g	1 oz
Water	¼ pint +3 tbsp	125 ml +3 tbsp	⅝ cup +3 tbsp
Malt extract	3 oz	75 g	3 tbsp
Black treacle	2 tbsp	2 tbsp	2 tbsp
Butter	1 oz	25 g	2 tbsp

Cream yeast in lukewarm water. Warm malt extract, treacle and butter together, mix and cool. Add cooled liquid and yeast liquid to dry ingredients and work to a soft dough. Turn on to a lightly floured board and knead. Divide in two, flatten each piece into an oblong the same width as tin and roll up like a Swiss roll. Place in two greased 1 lb/450 g loaf tins. Place tins in lightly greased polythene bags and leave to rise until dough doubles in size. Remove polythene. Bake at 400 °F/200 °C/Gas Mark 6 for 45 minutes. Brush tops of hot loaves with a wet brush dipped in honey. Cool on a wire tray.

Cidernuts

	Imperial	Metric	American
Plain flour	8 oz	225 g	2 cups
Pinch of salt			
Margarine	1 oz	25 g	2 tbsp
Fresh Yeast **or**	½ oz	15 g	½ oz
Dried yeast	¼ oz	8 g	¼ oz
Cider	¼ pint	125 ml	⅝ cup
Mincemeat	2 tbsp	2 tbsp	2 tbsp
Deep fat/oil to fry			
Caster sugar	4 oz	100 g	½ cup
Ground cinnamon	½ tsp	½ tsp	½ tsp

Sieve flour and salt together. Rub in margarine. Blend yeast with 2 teaspoons of cider and leave until frothy. Add to flour with remaining cider which has been warmed. Mix to form a soft dough. Knead lightly and cover with greased polythene. Leave to rise for 20 minutes in a warm place. Knead until smooth. Divide into 12 balls. Make a deep hole in each, and put ½ teaspoon mincemeat in each hole. Draw up edges to cover mincemeat. Place on a baking tray, cover with greased polythene and leave in a warm place until doubled in size. Fry in hot deep fat for 10 minutes, turning occasionally, until golden brown. Drain on kitchen paper. Mix together sugar and cinnamon and use to coat cidernuts.

Devonshire Splits

	Imperial	Metric	American
Strong plain flour	1 lb	450 g	4 cups
Salt	1 tsp	1 tsp	1 tsp
Milk	½ pint	250 ml	1¼ cups
Butter	2 oz	50 g	4 tbsp
Caster sugar	1 oz	25 g	2 tbsp
Fresh yeast **or**	½ oz	15 g	½ oz
Dried yeast	¼ oz	8 g	¼ oz
Strawberry jam			
Whipping cream	½ pint	250 ml	1¼ cups
Sifted icing sugar			

Sift flour and salt into a mixing bowl. Place milk in a saucepan with butter and half the sugar and heat to blood temperature. Cream fresh yeast with remaining sugar until liquid. If using dried yeast, follow directions on the packet. Make a well in the centre of dry ingredients, pour in yeast and milk, beat well to form an elastic dough, and knead until smooth. Cover with greased polythene, leave in a warm, not hot, place and allow to rise until doubled in size. Turn on to a lightly floured board, divide into 16 even-sized pieces and knead each one lightly into a ball. Place on greased baking trays and flatten slightly. Prove for about 20 minutes and bake at 425 °F/220°C/ Gas Mark 7 for 15—20 minutes. Allow to cool. Before serving, split buns and spread with strawberry jam and whipped or clotted cream. Dust the tops with icing sugar.

Chapter Two

SWEET AND SAVOURY TEABREADS

Not all 'breads' need to be made with yeast. These teabreads are half-way to being cakes, and are traditionally sliced and served with butter. They are ideal for those who do not like sweet cakes but fancy something a little more exciting than plain bread for some occasions. Bake these teabreads in a moderate oven, cool on a wire rack and slice them while still fresh.

Cottage Cheese Teabread

	Imperial	Metric	American
Cottage cheese	8 oz	225 g	1 cup
Soft brown sugar	4 oz	100 g	1 cup
Eggs	3	3	3
Walnuts	2 oz	50 g	½ cup
Celery sticks	2	2	2
Self-raising flour or flour sifted with 2 tsp baking powder	8 oz	225 g	2 cups
Baking powder	1 tsp	1 tsp	1 tsp

Sieve the cottage cheese. Cream with sugar and eggs and stir in chopped walnuts and celery. Sieve flour and baking powder and fold into mixture. Put into a greased and lined 2 lb/1 kg loaf tin. Bake at 350 °F/180 °C/Gas Mark 4 for 50 minutes. Leave in the tin for 5 minutes before turning out. Serve sliced and buttered.

25

Cheese and Walnut Loaf

	Imperial	Metric	American
Self-raising flour or flour sifted with 2 tsp baking powder	8 oz	225 g	2 cups
Dry mustard powder	1 tsp	1 tsp	1 tsp
Salt	1 tsp	1 tsp	1 tsp
Pepper			
Margarine	3 oz	75 g	6 tbsp
Cheddar cheese	4 oz	100 g	1 cup
Walnuts	1 oz	25 g	1/3 cup
Eggs	2	2	2
Cold water	1/4 pint	125 ml	5/8 cup

Sieve the flour, mustard and seasoning into a bowl and rub in the fat until the mixture resembles fine breadcrumbs. Stir in the grated cheese and chopped walnuts. Beat the eggs and milk together and add to the dry ingredients to give a soft dropping consistency. Place the mixture into a greased 1 lb/450 g loaf tin, smooth the top and bake in the centre of oven at 350 °F/180 °C/Gas Mark 4 for ¾—1 hour until golden brown and cooked through. Cool on a wire tray. Serve sliced with butter.

Farmhouse Tea Loaf

	Imperial	Metric	American
Mixed dried fruit	4 oz	100 g	1 cup
Caster sugar	4 oz	100 g	½ cup
Hot tea	¼ pint	125 ml	½ cup
Marmalade	2 tbsp	2 tbsp	2 tbsp
Egg	1	1	1
Self-raising flour or flour sifted with 2 tsp baking powder	8 oz	225 g	2 cups

Place the fruit, sugar and tea in a bowl. Leave to stand for at least 6 hours, but preferably overnight. Add the marmalade, egg and flour then mix well. Turn the mixture into prepared 1 lb/450 g loaf tin and bake at 350 °F/180 °C/Gas Mark 4 for about 50—60 minutes, until cooked. Cool and serve thinly sliced, and spread with butter.

Bran Loaf

	Imperial	Metric	American
All-Bran cereal	4 oz	100 g	1 cup
Sugar	5 oz	125 g	⅔ cup
Mixed dried fruit	8 oz	225 g	1¼ cups
Milk	½ pint	250 ml	1¼ cups
Self-raising flour or flour sifted with 1 tsp baking powder	4 oz	100 g	1 cup

Put cereal, sugar and fruit into a basin and stir in milk. Leave to stand for at least 30 minutes. Sieve in the flour, mix well and pour into a well-greased 2 lb/1 kg loaf tin. Bake at 350 °F/180 °C/Gas Mark 4 for 1¼ hours. Turn out on wire rack to cool.

Banana Teabread

	Imperial	Metric	American
Plain flour	8 oz	225 g	2 cups
Baking powder	3 tsp	3 tsp	3 tsp
Pinch of salt			
Margarine	2 oz	50 g	4 tbsp
Sugar	2 oz	50 g	¼ cup
Grated rind of lemon	1	1	1
Ripe bananas	3	3	3
Egg	1	1	1
A little milk			

Sieve flour, baking powder and salt. Rub in margarine. Add sugar, lemon rind and mashed bananas, and mix with egg and enough milk to give a soft batter. Put into a greased and floured 1 lb/450 g loaf tin. Bake at 375 °F/190 °C/Gas Mark 5 for 45 minutes. Cool on a wire rack. Serve sliced and buttered.

Hasty Cheese Loaf

	Imperial	Metric	American
Plain flour	8 oz	225 g	2 cups
Baking powder	1½ tsp	1½ tsp	1½ tsp
Salt	¼ tsp	¼ tsp	¼ tsp
Grated cheese	2 oz	50 g	½ cup
Milk			

Mix flour, baking powder, salt and cheese and add enough milk to make a soft dough. Form into 2 round cakes and put on a greased baking tray. Bake at 450 °F/230 °C/Gas Mark 8 for 10 minutes. Split, butter and eat while hot.

Welsh Fruit Loaf

	Imperial	Metric	American
Self-raising flour or flour sifted with 4 tsp baking powder	1 lb	450 g	4 cups
Butter or margarine	4 oz	100 g	½ cup
Salt	¼ tsp	¼ tsp	¼ tsp
Ground mixed spice	1 tsp	1 tsp	1 tsp
Sugar	4 oz	100 g	½ cup
Lemon	1	1	1
Sultanas	8 oz	225 g	2 cups
Black treacle	4 oz	100 g	4 tbsp
Egg	1	1	1
Milk	8 fl oz	200 ml	1 cup
Bicarbonate of soda	1 tsp	1 tsp	1 tsp

Rub the fat into the flour and stir in the salt, spice, sugar, grated lemon rind and sultanas. Mix and add the lemon juice, treacle, egg and most of the milk. Add the bicarbonate of soda to the milk and beat into the mixture. Put into a greased 2 lb/1 kg loaf tin. Bake at 325 °F/170 °C/Gas Mark 3 for 2 hours. Turn out on a wire rack to cool. Serve sliced and buttered.

Wholemeal Treacle Loaf

	Imperial	Metric	American
Wholemeal flour	8 oz	225 g	2 cups
Plain flour	8 oz	225 g	2 cups
Sugar	4 oz	100 g	½ cup
Seedless raisins	5 oz	125 g	1½ cups
Mixed nuts	1 oz	25 g	¼ cup
Black treacle	6 oz	150 g	6 tbsp
Milk	½ pint	250 ml	1¼ cups
Bicarbonate of soda	1 tsp	1 tsp	1 tsp
Egg	1	1	1

Stir wholemeal and plain flour together and add the sugar, raisins and chopped nuts. Heat treacle and milk until lukewarm. Add soda and pour into the flour. Add the beaten egg. Mix well and put into two greased 1 lb/450 g loaf tins. Bake at 350 °F/180 °C/Gas Mark 4 for 1 hour. Slice while still warm and spread with butter.

Peanut Loaf

	Imperial	Metric	American
Peanut butter	6 oz	150 g	¾ cup
Soft brown sugar	8 oz	225 g	1 cup
Egg	1	1	1
Milk	½ pint	250 ml	1¼ cups
Self-raising flour or flour sifted with 4 tsp baking powder	1 lb	450 g	4 cups
Salt	1 tsp	1 tsp	1 tsp
Salted peanuts	2 oz	50 g	⅓ cup

Cream the peanut butter and sugar together until well blended. Beat the egg and milk together lightly and add alternately to the creamed mixture with the flour and salt. Mix well and stir in the chopped peanuts. Put into a greased 2 lb/1 kg loaf tin. Bake at 375 °F/190 °C/Gas Mark 5 for 1½ hours.

Chapter Three

SCONES AND GIRDLE CAKES

Small plain scones and girdle cakes are a traditional part of the tea-table, but they are just as good for breakfast or snacks. Scones are made with a soft dough which is cut and rolled, then baked in a hot oven. The old-fashioned way of cooking them, before the coming of baking-ovens, was on a thick plate of iron over a hot fire. This implement was called a girdle, or griddle, and can still be obtained for cooking scones over an electric, gas or solid fuel stove. A solid electric hotplate may be used instead, or a thick frying pan. This method of cooking is preferred for 'drop' scones made with a thick creamy batter.

Scone Ring

	Imperial	Metric	American
Self-raising flour or flour sifted with 2 tsp baking powder	8 oz	225 g	2 cups
Pinch of salt			
Margarine	2 oz	50 g	¼ cup
Sugar	2 oz	50 g	¼ cup
Mixed dried fruit	2 oz	50 g	½ cup
Egg	1	1	1
Milk	6 tbsp	6 tbsp	6 tbsp

Sieve flour and salt into bowl and rub in margarine. Add sugar and dried fruit. Beat egg with milk. Add most of liquid to the mixture to make a fairly soft dough. Divide dough into 8 and lightly knead each piece into a round. Place scones overlapping to form a ring on a greased baking tray. Brush the top only with remaining milk and egg liquid. Bake at 425 °F/220 °C/Gas Mark 7 for about 20—25 minutes until golden brown and cooked through. Cool on a wire tray.

Breakfast Scones

	Imperial	Metric	American
Plain flour	8 oz	225 g	2 cups
Salt	1 tsp	1 tsp	1 tsp
Baking powder	3 tsp	3 tsp	3 tsp
Sugar	2 oz	50 g	¼ cup
Butter or margarine	4 oz	100 g	½ cup
Seedless raisins	4 oz	100 g	1 cup
Egg	1	1	1
Milk (scant measure)	½ pint	250 ml	1¼ cups

Sieve together flour, salt, baking powder and sugar. Cut and rub in lard, add raisins. Beat egg lightly and add milk. Mix flour to soft dough, turn on to floured board and knead lightly. Divide dough in half, roll each section into ½ in/1.25 cm thick rounds. Cut each round into 6 wedges and place on greased baking sheet. Brush tops with milk and sprinkle with sugar. Bake at 450 °F/230 °C/Gas Mark 8 for 15 minutes. Serve hot with butter.

Drop Scones

	Imperial	Metric	American
Plain flour	8 oz	225 g	2 cups
Salt	¼ tsp	¼ tsp	¼ tsp
Bicarbonate of soda	½ tsp	½ tsp	½ tsp
Cream of tartar	1 tsp	1 tsp	1 tsp
Caster sugar	1 tbsp	1 tbsp	1 tbsp
Egg	1	1	1
Milk	¼ pint	125 ml	⅝ cup
Butter or margarine	1 oz	25 g	2 tbsp

Sieve flour, soda and cream of tartar. Stir in the sugar. Mix to a thick batter with egg and milk, and stir in melted fat. Grease a hot girdle or thick frying pan lightly. Drop on the mixture in spoonfuls. When bubbles appear on the surface, turn quickly and cook the other side. Put in the folds of a clean teacloth to keep soft while cooling.

Girdle Scones

	Imperial	Metric	American
Self-raising flour or flour sifted with 2 tsp baking powder	8 oz	225 g	2 cups
Salt	½ tsp	½ tsp	½ tsp
Baking powder	1 tsp	1 tsp	1 tsp
Caster sugar	2 tsp	2 tsp	2 tsp
Egg	1	1	1
Black treacle or molasses	2 tbsp	2 tbsp	2 tbsp
Cold milk	½ pint	250 ml	1¼ cups

Sift dry ingredients into a bowl. Make a well in the centre. Drop in egg and treacle or molasses, then gradually mix to a thick batter with the milk, drawing in flour from sides of the bowl. Beat with the back of a wooden spoon till batter is smooth and creamy; then drop spoonfuls on to a well-greased girdle, thick frying pan or hot plate of an electric cooker. Cook for ¾—1 minute on each side. Pile scones in a folded napkin as they are cooked, then serve warm with butter.

Welsh Cakes

	Imperial	Metric	American
Self-raising flour or flour sifted with 2 tsp baking powder	8 oz	225 g	2 cups
Butter	5 oz	125 g	¾ cup
Sugar	4 oz	100 g	½ cup
Currants	3 oz	75 g	¾ cup
Sultanas	2 oz	50 g	½ cup
Ground ginger	¼ tsp	¼ tsp	¼ tsp
Grated lemon rind	½ tsp	½ tsp	½ tsp
Egg	1	1	1

A little milk to mix

Rub the butter into the flour. Stir in the sugar, dried fruit, ginger and lemon rind. Mix to a firm dough with the egg and a little milk is necessary. Roll out and cut into rounds with a scone cutter. Bake at 400 °F/200 °C/Gas Mark 6 for 15 minutes. Sprinkle with a little sugar while still warm. Serve freshly baked.

Chapter Four

CAKES

Cakes may be made by rubbing in, creaming or whisking. In simple terms, the fat may be rubbed in to the flour to give a breadcrumb-like mixture which is made into a dough with liquid; or the fat and sugar are creamed together before the other ingredients are added. Very light cakes are made by whisking eggs and sugar together before adding the other ingredients. An electric mixer may be used for all these cake-making operations, but it is important not to over-mix cakes or they become sad and heavy.

Be sure to use the ingredients specified, whether plain or self-raising flour, and the correct type of sugar. Also be sure to use the size of tin indicated in the recipe, or else the cooking time will be affected by the different depth of the cake, and you may get a crusty outside and a raw interior. When you have made a few cakes, you can begin to experiment with different flavourings, and can pair the cakes with a variety of icings and fillings.

Plain Cake
(Rubbed in method)

	Imperial	Metric	American
Plain flour	8 oz	225 g	2 cups
Baking powder	2 tsp	2 tsp	2 tsp
Pinch of salt			
Butter or margarine	3 oz	75 g	⅓ cup
Sugar	3 oz	75 g	⅓ cup
Egg	1	1	1
Milk	¼ pint	125 ml	⅝ cup
Flavouring			

Sieve together the flour, baking powder and salt. Rub in the fat until the mixture is like breadcrumbs. Add the sugar, and work in the egg and milk to make a soft dropping consistency. Add any other flavourings or ingredients. Put into a greased 7 in/17.5 cm round deep tin. Bake at 375 °F/190 °C/Gas Mark 5 for 50 minutes. For a **fruit cake,** add 4 oz/100 g/1 cup mixed dried fruit. For a **chocolate cake,** add 1½ oz/40 g/¼ cup cocoa and a few drops of vanilla essence.

Rubbed in Method

1. Sift flour, salt, any raising agent and spices into a bowl.
2. Cut fat into small pieces.
3. Add fat to dry ingredients and rub with the tips of the fingers until the mixture looks like coarse breadcrumbs.
4. Add remaining ingredients and mix until smooth.

Rich Cake (Creamed Method)

	Imperial	Metric	American
Butter or margarine	6 oz	150 g	¾ cup
Caster sugar	5 oz	125 g	10 tbsp
Plain flour	8 oz	225 g	2 cups
Baking powder	1 tsp	1 tsp	1 tsp
Eggs	3	3	3

Cream the fat and sugar together with a wooden spoon or electric mixer until the mixture is light and fluffy with no grittiness. Sieve the flour and baking powder. Add a little flour to the creamed mixture, then beat in the eggs one at a time. Fold in the rest of the flour and any flavouring or additional ingredient. Put into a greased 8 in/20 cm round deep tin. Bake at 350 °F/180 °C/Gas Mark 4 for 1¼ hours. For **fruit cake,** add 12 oz/350 g mixed dried fruit. For **coconut cake,** add 2 oz/50 g desiccated coconut.

Creamed Method

1. Have fat at room temperature so that it is soft but not melted.
2. Add sugar and beat with a wooden spoon or an electric mixer until the mixture is very soft and fluffy like whipped cream.
3. Add dry ingredients and any specified liquids and flavourings.

Fatless Sponge

	Imperial	Metric	American
Eggs	4	4	4
Caster sugar	4 oz	100 g	½ cup
Pinch of salt			
Plain flour	4 oz	100 g	1 cup

Whisk the eggs, sugar and salt until light, thick and creamy. Fold in sieved flour. Put into two greased and floured 8 in/20 cm sandwich tins or round shallow pans. Bake at 400 °F/200 °C/Gas Mark 6 for 20 minutes. Cool on a wire rack and put together with jam. Sprinkle caster or icing sugar on top.

Everyday Gingerbread

	Imperial	Metric	American
Margarine	4 oz	100 g	½ cup
Black treacle	6 oz	150 g	6 tbsp
Golden syrup	2 oz	50 g	2 tbsp
Milk	¼ pint	125 ml	⅝ cup
Eggs	2	2	2
Plain flour	8 oz	225 g	2 cups
Sugar	2 oz	50 g	¼ cup
Ground mixed spice	1 tsp	1 tsp	1 tsp
Bicarbonate of soda	1 tsp	1 tsp	1 tsp
Ground ginger	2 tsps	2 tsps	2 tsps

Using a large saucepan, warm together
margarine, black treacle and syrup. Add milk and
allow to cool. Beat eggs and blend with cooled
mixture. Sieve dry ingredients together into a bowl,
add the cooled mixture and blend in with a
tablespoon. Turn into a greased and lined 7 in/17.5 cm
square tin. Bake at 300 °F/150 °C/Gas Mark 2, for
1¼—1½ hours. **For a change,** add 4 oz/100 g/1 cup
chopped dried figs or dates, or add 1 oz/25 g each
sultanas, crystallized ginger and chopped almonds.

Victoria Sandwich

	Imperial	Metric	American
Margarine	4 oz	100 g	½ cup
Caster sugar	4 oz	100 g	½ cup
Eggs	2	2	2
Self-raising flour or flour sifted with 1 tsp baking powder	4 oz	100 g	1 cup
Jam			
Caster or icing sugar			

Cream the fat and sugar together until light and fluffy and almost white. Add the eggs one at a time and beat well. Fold in the sieved flour and put the mixture into two greased and floured 7 in/17.5 cm sandwich tins or round shallow pans. Bake at 375 °F 190 °C/Gas Mark 5 for 25 minutes. Cool on a wire rack. Put the cakes together with jam and sprinkle the top with sugar.

Swiss Roll

	Imperial	Metric	American
Eggs	3	3	3
Caster sugar	4½ oz	115 g	½ cup + 2 tsps
Plain flour	3 oz	75 g	¾ cup
Baking powder	½ tsp	½ tsp	½ tsp
Cold water	1 tbsp	1 tbsp	1 tbsp
Jam			

Beat eggs and sugar until light and fluffy. Fold in flour sifted with baking powder, and the water. Spread evenly in a greased and lined Swiss roll tin. Bake at 400 °F/200 °C/Gas Mark 6 for 10 minutes. Turn out on a sugared paper, trim edges with a sharp knife. Spread quickly with just warm jam and roll up tightly. Sprinkle with caster sugar before serving.

Yorkshire Parkin

	Imperial	Metric	American
Plain flour	6 oz	150 g	1½ cups
Salt	1 tsp	1 tsp	1 tsp
Ground ginger	1 tsp	1 tsp	1 tsp
Ground cinnamon	2 tsps	2 tsps	2 tsps
Bicarbonate of soda	1 tsp	1 tsp	1 tsp
Medium oatmeal	10 oz	275 g	1⅔ cups
Black treacle or molasses	6 oz	150 g	6 tbsps
Butter	5 oz	125 g	⅔ cup
Soft brown sugar	4 oz	100 g	½ cup
Milk	¼ pint	125 ml	⅔ cup
Egg	1	1	1

Sieve together the flour, salt, spices and soda, and stir in the oatmeal. Put the treacle, butter, sugar and milk into a saucepan and heat gently until the butter has melted. Cool to lukewarm and beat in the egg. Pour into the centre of the dry ingredients and beat until smooth. Put into a greased and lined 7 in/17.5 cm square tin. Bake at 350 °F/180 °C/Gas Mark 4 for 1 hour. Keep in an airtight tin for 2 weeks before using.

Chocolate Sponge Cake

	Imperial	Metric	American
Self-raising flour or flour sifted with 1½ tsp baking powder	6 oz	150 g	1½ cups
Salt	¼ tsp	¼ tsp	¼ tsp
Eggs	2	2	2
Soft margarine	6 oz	150 g	¾ cup
Caster sugar	6 oz	150 g	¾ cup
Cocoa	1 tbsp	1 tbsp	1 tbsp
Warm water	1 tbsp	1 tbsp	1 tbsp
Icing			
Cocoa	1 tbsp	1 tbsp	1 tbsp
Water	1 tbsp	1 tbsp	1 tbsp
Butter	2 oz	50 g	¼ cup
Icing sugar	4 oz	100 g	½ cup

Heat oven to 350 °F/180 °C/Gas Mark 4. Place all ingredients in mixing bowl. Beat for 3 minutes, using a wooden spoon. Divide mixture between two greased 7 in/17.5 cm sandwich tins or round shallow pans. Bake for 25—30 minutes. Remove from tins and cool on wire rack. Mix cocoa and water in small pan over low heat, until smooth. Bring to boil, then cool. Cream butter, then gradually beat in icing sugar. Beat in cocoa mixture. Spread half the icing on one cake and sandwich the two cakes together. Cover top with remainder of icing and, using a large fork, make a zigzag pattern. Sprinkle with a little icing sugar. Leave icing to set firmly.

Yogurt Cake

	Imperial	Metric	American
Plain flour	6 oz	150 g	1½ cups
Bicarbonate of soda	2 tsps	2 tsps	2 tsps
Salt	½ tsp	½ tsp	½ tsp
Butter	2 oz	50 g	¼ cup
Caster sugar	11 oz	325 g	1½ cups
Eggs	3	3	3
Natural yogurt	¼ pint	125 ml	⅝ cup
Grated rind of 1 lemon			

Icing

Icing sugar	2 oz	50 g	¼ cup
Grated rind of 1 lemon			
Lemon juice	2 tbsp	2 tbsp	2 tbsp

Grease and flour an 8 in/20 cm round deep cake tin. Sift together flour, bicarbonate of soda, and salt. Cream butter until soft. Add sugar and beaten egg yolks and mix thoroughly. The mixture will be very crumbly at this stage. Add yogurt and lemon rind and beat well. Gradually stir in sifted flour. Whisk egg whites until just stiff and carefully fold into yogurt mixture. Pour into cake tin and bake at 350 °F/180 °C/Gas Mark 4 for 1 hour 15 minutes. Turn out on to a cooling tray. To make icing, mix icing sugar with lemon rind and juice. Pour over top of cake and leave to set. This cake is nicer when eaten the following day.

Honey Fruit Cake

	Imperial	Metric	American
Self-raising flour or flour sifted with 1½ tsps baking powder	12 oz	350 g	3 cups
Ground mixed spice	1 tsp	1 tsp	1 tsp
Soft margarine	6 oz	150 g	¾ cup
Soft light brown sugar	4 oz	100 g	½ cup
Clear honey	3 tbsp	3 tbsp	3 tbsp
Sultanas and raisins	6 oz	150 g	1½ cups
Glacé cherries	4 oz	100 g	1 cup
Walnut halves	4 oz	100 g	1 cup
Eggs	3	3	3

Set oven at 350 °F/180 °C/Gas Mark 4. Grease and line an 8 in/20 cm round deep cake tin. Cut cherries in quarters and chop walnuts, reserving 8 halves. Beat all the ingredients, except the reserved walnut halves, together for 2 minutes, using a wooden spoon. Put into the tin and arrange the reserved walnut halves on top of the cake. Place in centre of oven and bake for 1½ hours. Leave to cool slightly in tin before turning out.

Apple and Clove Cake

	Imperial	Metric	American
Self-raising flour or flour sifted with 2 tsps baking powder	8 oz	225 g	2 cups
Pinch of salt			
Ground cloves	½ tsp	½ tsp	½ tsp
Butter or margarine	4 oz	100 g	½ cup
Soft brown sugar	4 oz	100 g	½ cup
Raisins	2 oz	50 g	½ cup
Cooking apples	8 oz	225 g	1½ cups
Eggs	2	2	2
Demerara sugar	1 oz	25 g	2 tbsp

Sift flour, salt and ground cloves into a mixing bowl. Rub in fat until mixture resembles fine breadcrumbs. Stir in sugar and raisins. Peel, core and slice apples. Add to mixture. Lightly beat eggs and add to mixture. Beat until smooth for about 1 minute. Turn into a greased and lined 9½ x 5½ x 3 in/24 x 14 x 8 cm loaf tin and sprinkle with demerara sugar. Bake at 300 °F/150 °C/Gas Mark 2 for 1½—1¾ hours until topping is golden brown and cake is firm to touch. Turn out and cool on a wire tray. Serve warm or cold, sliced, and buttered if liked.

Spiced Walnut Ring

	Imperial	Metric	American
Margarine	5 oz	125 g	10 tblsps
Soft brown sugar	2 oz	50 g	¼ cup
Clear honey	3 tbsp	3 tbsp	3 tbsp
Eggs	2	2	2
Self-raising flour sifted			
with 1½ tsp baking powder	6 oz	150 g	1½ cups
Ground mixed spice	2 tsps	2 tsps	2 tsps
Ground cinnamon	½ tsp	½ tsp	½ tsp
Chopped walnuts	3 oz	75 g	1 cup

Cream the margarine, sugar and honey together. Gradually beat in the eggs. Sieve the flour, mixed spice and cinnamon. Fold in the walnuts and flour. Place in a greased ring mould (capacity 2¼—2½ pint/1—1.5 litre), level the surface and bake at 350 °F/180 °C/Gas Mark 4 for approximately 40 minutes until well risen, firm to touch and beginning to shrink from the edge of the mould. Cool on a wire rack. Cover with glacé icing and decorate with walnut halves if desired.

Crumble Cake

	Imperial	Metric	American
Plain flour	8 oz	225 g	2 cups
Sugar	4 oz	100 g	½ cup
Margarine	6 oz	150 g	¾ cup
Grated lemon rind	2 tsps	2 tsps	2 tsps

Stir sugar into flour and rub in fat until the mixture looks like fine breadcrumbs. Stir in grated peel. Put into shallow 8 in/20 cm tin and press down very lightly. Bake at 325 °F/170 °C/Gas Mark 3 for 30 minutes. Leave in tin until cold and cut into slices.

Slab Fruit Cake

	Imperial	Metric	American
Self-raising flour or flour sifted with 2½ tsps baking powder	10 oz	300 g	2½ cups
Ground mixed spice	2 tsps	2 tsps	2 tsps
Salt	1 tsp	1 tsp	1 tsp
Butter	5 oz	125 g	10 tbsp
Soft brown sugar	5 oz	125 g	10 tbsp
Large eggs	2	2	2
Milk	4 tbsp	4 tbsp	4 tbsp
Mixed dried fruit	1 lb	450 g	2 cups

Sieve flour, spice and salt. Rub in butter and stir in sugar. Add beaten eggs and milk and stir in the dried fruit. Mix well and put into a greased 7 x 11 in/17.5 x 27.5 cm tin. Bake at 350 °F/180 °C/Gas Mark 4 for 1 hour. Cool in the tin and cut into squares.

Cherry Lemon Cake

	Imperial	Metric	American
Self-raising flour or flour sifted with 3 tsp baking powder	12 oz	350 g	3 cups
Pinch of salt			
Butter	6 oz	150 g	¾ cup
Caster sugar	6 oz	150 g	¾ cup
Glacé cherries	4 oz	100 g	⅔ cup
Eggs	2	2	2
Grated rind of ½ lemon, Milk			

Sieve flour and salt and rub in butter. Stir in sugar, quartered cherries and lemon rind. Beat in eggs and add a little milk to give a dropping consistency. Put into greased 2 lb/1 kg loaf tin. Bake at 350 °F/180 °C/Gas Mark 4 for 1¼ hours. Cool on a rack.

Easy Farmhouse Cake

	Imperial	Metric	American
Soft margarine	6 oz	150 g	1½ cups
Caster sugar	6 oz	150 g	¾ cup
Eggs	3	3	3
Milk	3 tbsp	3 tbsp	3 tbsp
Sultanas	3 oz	75 g	1 cup
Raisins	3 oz	75 g	1 cup
Glacé cherries	3 oz	75 g	½ cup
Self-raising flour or flour sifted with baking powder	12 oz	350 g	3 cups
Ground mixed spice	1 tsp	1 tsp	1 tsp

Put all the ingredients together into a mixing bowl and beat well for about 3 minutes until well mixed. Put into a greased and lined 8 in/20 cm round deep cake tin. Bake at 350 °F/180 °C/Gas Mark 4 for 1½ hours. Leave in the tin for 5 minutes and then turn out on a wire rack to cool.

Eggless Cake

	Imperial	Metric	American
Plain	12 oz	350 g	3 cups
Ground nutmeg	½ tsp	½ tsp	½ tsp
Bicarbonate of soda	¾ tsp	¾ tsp	¾ tsp
Cream of tartar	1½ tsps	1½ tsps	1½ tsps
Soft brown sugar	6 oz	150 g	¾ cup
Margarine	6 oz	150 g	¾ cup
Seedless raisins	12 oz	350 g	2 cups
Milk			

Stir together all dry ingredients and rub in fat. Stir in raisins and mix to a stiff dough with a little milk. Put into greased 10 in/25 cm cake tin and bake at 350 °F/180 °C/Gas Mark 4 for 1¾ hours. Cool on a rack.

Dripping Cake

	Imperial	Metric	American
Self-raising flour or flour sifted with 2 tsp baking powder	8 oz	225 g	2 cups
Baking powder	1 tsp	1 tsp	1 tsp
Beef dripping	4 oz	100 g	¼ lb
Soft brown sugar	4 oz	100 g	½ cup
Egg	1	1	1
Milk	3 tbsp	3 tbsp	3 tbsp
Currants	8 oz	225 g	2½-3 cups

Sieve the flour and baking powder together. Cream the dripping and work in the sugar. Cream again until soft and light. Add a little of the flour alternately with the egg and milk until all the flour has been used. Beat well and fold in the currants. Put into a greased and floured 7 in/17.5 cm round deep cake tin. Bake at 325 °F/170 °C/Gas Mark 3 for 1¼ hours. Cool on a wire rack.

Boiled Fruit Cake

	Imperial	Metric	American
Butter or margarine	5 oz	125 g	10 tbsp
Golden syrup	6 tbsp	6 tbsp	6 tbsp
Milk	¼ pint	125 ml	½ cup
Dates	4 oz	100 g	1 cup
Currants	8 oz	225 g	2½-3 cups
Sultanas	4 oz	100 g	1-1½ cups
Seedless raisins	8 oz	225 g	2 cups
Chopped mixed peel	4 oz	100 g	1 cup
Self-raising flour or flour sifted with 2 tsp baking powder	8 oz	225 g	2 cups
Ground mixed spice	1 tsp	1 tsp	1 tsp
Ground nutmeg	1 tsp	1 tsp	1 tsp
Pinch of salt			
Eggs	2	2	2
Bicarbonate of soda	½ tsp	½ tsp	½ tsp

Put the fat, syrup, milk, chopped dates, dried fruit and peel into a saucepan, and heat slowly until the fat has melted. Simmer gently for 5 minutes, stirring once or twice, and then cool completely. Sieve together the flour, spices and salt. Make a well in the centre and add the eggs but do not stir. Add the soda to the fruit mixture and stir well. Pour on to the flour, mix thoroughly and beat well. Pour into a greased and lined 10 in/25 cm round deep cake tin. Bake in a moderate oven 325 °F/170 °C/Gas Mark 3 for 1¾ hours. This is a rich moist cake which keeps well and is particularly good for packed meals.

Dundee Cake

	Imperial	Metric	American
Butter	8 oz	225 g	1 cup
Caster sugar	8 oz	225 g	1 cup
Eggs	5	5	5
Self-raising flour or flour sifted with 2 tsp baking powder	8 oz	225 g	2 cups
Ground nutmeg	½ tsp	½ tsp	½ tsp
Mixed currants and sultanas	12 oz	350 g	3 cups
Glacé cherries	3 oz	75 g	1 cup
Chopped mixed peel	2 oz	50 g	¾ cup
Ground almonds	3 oz	75 g	¾ cup
Blanched almonds	2 oz	50 g	½ cup

Cream the butter and sugar until light and fluffy. Add the eggs one at a time with a little flour to prevent curdling. Beat well after each addition. Stir in most of the flour and then the dried fruit, chopped cherries and peel, lightly coated with the remaining flour. Stir in the ground almonds. Put into a greased and lined 10 in/25 cm round deep tin. Bake in a moderate oven, 325 °F/170 °C/Gas Mark 3 for 2½ hours. Halfway through cooking time, sprinkle split blanched almonds on top.

Sugar and Spice Cake

	Imperial	Metric	American
Butter or margarine	4 oz	100 g	½ cup
Sugar	6 oz	150 g	¾ cup
Eggs	2	2	2
Hot water	4 tbsp	4 tbsp	4 tbsp
Plain flour	10 oz	300 g	2½ cups
Bicarbonate of soda	1 tsp	1 tsp	1 tsp
Raspberry or apricot jam	8 oz	225 g	8 tbsp
Ground mixed spice	1 tsp	1 tsp	1 tsp
Orange glacé icing	½ tsp	½ tsp	½ tsp

Cream the fat and sugar together until light and fluffy. Add the eggs whole, beating thoroughly after each addition, then stir in the water. Fold in the sifted dry ingredients alternately with the jam and beat thoroughly to blend all the ingredients. Pour the mixture into a round fluted cake tin and bake in a moderate oven, 325 °F/180 °C/Gas Mark 3, for 1 hour until the cake is well risen and firm. Turn out, cool and ice.

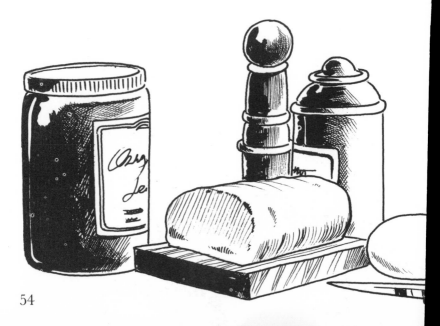

Quick Orange Cake

	Imperial	Metric	American
Butter	4 oz	100 g	½ cup
Caster sugar	8 oz	225 g	1 cup
Eggs	2	2	2
Orange juice	¼ pint	125 ml	½ cup
Plain flour	8 oz	225 g	2 cups
Baking powder	2 tsps	2 tsps	2 tsps
Salt	¼ tsp	¼ tsp	¼ tsp
Topping			
Grated rind of oranges	2	2	2
Sugar	1½ oz	40 g	3 tbsp

Cream the butter and sugar and work in the eggs and orange juice. Fold in the flour sieved with the baking powder and salt. Beat well and put into a greased 10 in/25 cm spring-form cake tin. Mix the orange rind and sugar and sprinkle on top of the cake mixture. Bake at 350 °F/180 °C/Gas Mark 4 for 1¼ hours. Open the sides of the tin and leave the cake to cool for 10 minutes, then put on to a wire rack until cold.

Orange Bran Cake

	Imperial	Metric	American
Butter or margarine	4 oz	100 g	½ cup
Caster sugar	4 oz	100 g	½ cup
Eggs	2	2	2
Grated rind of 1 orange			
Orange juice	4 tbsp	4 tbsp	4 tbsp
Self-raising flour sifted			
with 1½ tsp baking powder	6 oz	150 g	1½ cups
All-Bran cereal	2 oz	50 g	½ cup
Chopped mixed peel	1 oz	25 g	1 tblsp

Glacé icing (see page 92)

Cream the fat and sugar together until light and fluffy. Add the eggs gradually and beat the mixture well. Add the orange rind and juice, and stir in the flour, cereal and peel. Mix well and put into a greased 6 in/15 cm round deep cake tin. Bake at 350 °F/180 °C/Gas Mark 4 for 1 hour. Leave in the tin for 5 minutes and then turn on to a wire rack to cool. When cold, pour on glacé icing.

Battenburg Cake

	Imperial	Metric	American
Butter or margarine	6 oz	150 g	¾ cup
Caster sugar	6 oz	150 g	¾ cup
Eggs	3	3	3
Few drops of vanilla essence			
Self-raising flour or flour sifted with 1 tsp baking powder	8 oz	225 g	2 cups
Cochineal			
Butter icing	4 tbsp	4 tbsp	4 tbsp
Jam	4 tbsp	4 tbsp	4 tbsp
Almond paste	8 oz	225 g	½ lb
A little caster sugar			

Grease and line a square 7 in/17.5 cm cake tin. Fold a piece of greaseproof or non-stick baking paper into several thicknesses and put across the centre of the tin to divide it into two equal parts. Cream the fat and sugar until light and fluffy and beat in the eggs a little at a time. Add the vanilla essence and the flour. Put half the mixture into one side of the tin. Add a little cochineal to the other half of the mixture, beat and put into the second half of the tin. Bake at 350 °F/180 °C/Gas Mark 4 for 35 minutes. Cool on a wire rack. Cut each piece of cake into two lengths. Sandwich together with butter icing to make a checked patterned cake. Warm the jam slightly and sieve. Spread round the long edges of the cake with a pastry brush. Roll the almond paste into a rectangle and cover the cake, leaving the checked ends showing. Score the top with a knife and pinch the two top edges with the fingers to give a decorative pattern. Sprinkle with caster sugar.

Cider Apple and Raisin Gateau

	Imperial	Metric	American
Cider	¾ pint	375 ml	1⅞ cups
Granulated sugar	5 oz	125 g	⅝ cup
Seedless raisins	4 oz	100 g	1 cup
Eggs	3	3	3
Caster sugar	3 oz	75 g	⅜ cup
Plain flour	2½ oz	65 g	10 tbsp
Cooking apple	1	1	1
Double cream	¼ pint	125 ml	½ cup

Put ½ pint/250 ml/1¼ cups cider, 4 oz/100 g/½ cup granulated sugar and 4 oz/100 g/1 cup raisins into a saucepan. Bring to the boil and reduce the liquid by half. Cool, cover and allow to stand overnight. Whisk the eggs and caster sugar in a large bowl over hot but not boiling water until thick. (The bubbles should be small and opaque and the mark of the whisk retained by the mixture.) Remove from the bowl and continue to whisk until cold. Fold in the sifted flour, a third at a time. Turn into two greased 7 in/17.5 cm layer cake tins and bake at 375 °F/190 °C/Gas Mark 5 for 15 minutes. Allow to cool in the tins for 5 minutes before turning on to a cake rack. Drain off the raisins, reserving the syrup. Peel, core and slice the apple. Poach very gently in the remaining cider and granulated sugar until just tender. Drain and cool. Whip the cream stiffly. Put one of the cake layers on a serving dish, brush with the reserved syrup. Spread half the whipped cream over the cake and cover with the raisins. Put the other cake layer on top, brush again with the reserved syrup (reserving 2 tablespoons). Arrange the poached apple slices on top.

Brush with the remaining syrup and decorate with the remaining whipped cream. Serve with forks as a special cake or as a dinner party pudding.

Devil's Food Cake

	Imperial	Metric	American
Plain flour	6 oz	150 g	1½ cups
Baking powder	¼ tsp	¼ tsp	¼ tsp
Bicarbonate of soda	1 tsp	1 tsp	1 tsp
Cocoa	2 oz	50 g	½ cup
Butter	4 oz	100 g	½ cup
Caster sugar	10 oz	300 g	1¼ cups
Eggs	2	2	2
Water	8 fl oz	200 ml	1 cup
Chocolate butter icing			

Sieve together the flour, baking powder, bicarbonate of soda and cocoa. Beat the butter until light and creamy and gradually beat in the sugar. Mix in the eggs, a little at a time, beating well. Fold in the flour alternately with the water. Put into two 8 in/20 cm greased sandwich tins or round shallow pans, bottom-lined with greaseproof or non-stick baking paper. Bake at 350 °F/180 °C/Gas Mark 4 for 1 hour. Turn out on a wire rack to cool. When cold, sandwich the cakes together with chocolate butter icing.

Christmas Cake

	Imperial	Metric	American
Butter or margarine	7 oz	175 g	14 tbsp
Soft brown sugar	7 oz	175 g	14 tbsp
Large eggs	3	3	3
Grated rind and juice of 1 lemon			
Currants	14 oz	400 g	3½ cups
Sultanas	7 oz	175 g	2 cups
Raisins	7 oz	175 g	2 cups
Glacé cherries	3 oz	75 g	1 cup
Mixed peel	1½ oz	40 g	½ cup
Blanched almonds	1½ oz	40 g	½ cup
Plain flour	7 oz	175 g	1¾ cups
Ground mixed spice	½ tsp	½ tsp	½ tsp
Brandy or sherry	2 tbsp	2 tbsp	2 tbsp
Clear honey	1 tbsp	1 tbsp	1 tbsp

Grease and line a deep 8 in/20 cm or 7 in/17.5 cm square cake tin. Cream the butter and sugar until light and fluffy. Beat in the eggs, one at a time, and add lemon rind. Add fruit and chopped nuts and mix together thoroughly. Stir in the flour, spice, lemon juice, brandy and honey, mixing well. Place the mixture in the prepared cake tin and smooth top with the back of a spoon. Place the cake on a double sheet of brown paper on the baking sheet. Bake on the middle shelf of oven at 325 °F/170 °C/Gas Mark 3 for 1 hour. Reduce heat to 300 °F/150 °C/Gas Mark 2 for a further 2½ hours. Cover cake with a sheet of paper, half way through cooking time, if it is getting too brown. When cooked, test with a skewer, which when pushed into the centre of the cake should come out clean. Remove cake to cool in tin, then turn out and remove paper. The cake can be wrapped in foil and stored in a cake tin, ready for being iced.

Almond Paste

	Imperial	Metric	American
Sugar	5 oz	125 g	10 tbsp
Icing sugar	5 oz	125 g	10 tbsp
Ground almonds	10 oz	275 g	2½ cups
Egg	1	1	1
Juice of ½ lemon			
Vanilla essence	¼ tsp	¼ tsp	¼ tsp
Almond essence	¼ tsp	¼ tsp	¼ tsp
Apricot jam			

Place sugars in a bowl, and add ground almonds, mixing well. Beat egg, lemon juice and flavouring together and pour on to dry ingredients. Mix with a fork to a pliable paste. Add a little more sieved icing sugar if paste is too sticky or a little lemon juice if too stiff. Roll out on to a sheet of greaseproof paper, dusted with icing sugar. Brush top of cake with boiled sieved apricot jam and place on almond paste, trimming neatly. Measure circumference of cake with a piece of string and re-roll paste to required width and length to fit sides of cake. Brush sides of cake with jam and roll cake along almond paste, carefully joining edge of top to edge of sides. Place on an upturned plate. Cover with greaseproof paper and leave to dry for 2—3 days before icing.

Royal Icing

	Imperial	Metric	American
Icing sugar	1¼ lb	500–625 g	2½ cups
Egg whites	3—4	3—4	3—4

Place the icing sugar in a bowl. Break up the egg whites with a fork, but do not beat. Gradually add the egg whites to the icing sugar, beating well, after each addition, and continue beating until icing is smooth.

Keep bowl of icing covered with a damp cloth, while it is being used, to prevent skin forming. To ice cake: Place a little icing in the centre of a cake board to secure cake and place cake centrally on board. Using a palette knife, spread icing over top of cake, working backwards and forwards with knife to remove any air bubbles. Using a well scrubbed ruler, smooth icing over the cake, by drawing the ruler towards you. Repeat to obtain a smooth surface. When dry, cover sides of cake, using a knife or plastic scraper to smooth the surface. Leave to dry and cover with a second coat. Decorate as desired.

Yule Log

	Imperial	Metric	American
Eggs	3	3	3
Caster sugar	3 oz	75 g	⅓ cup
Clear honey	1 tsp	1 tsp	1 tsp
Self-raising flour or flour sifted with ½ tsp baking powder	3 oz	75 g	¾ cup
Pinch of salt			
Cocoa	2 tsps	2 tsps	2 tsps
Drinking chocolate	1 oz	25 g	2 tbsp

Caster sugar			
Clear honey	*2 tbsp*	*2 tbsp*	*2 tbsp*
Butter Cream and Decoration			
Butter	*3 oz*	*75 g*	*⅓ cup*
Icing sugar, sieved	*8 oz*	*225 g*	*1 cup*
Milk	*1 tbsp*	*1 tbsp*	*1 tbsp*
Chocolate	*1 oz*	*25 g*	*1 oz*

Grease and line a Swiss roll tin. Prepare mixture by breaking the eggs into a bowl, add sugar and honey and stand over a saucepan of boiling water. Make sure that the bottom of the bowl does not touch the water. Whisk for at least 5 minutes until mixture is thick and creamy. Remove from heat and fold in sieved ingredients lightly with a metal spoon. Spread mixture evenly into the tin and bake at 425 °F/220 °C/Gas Mark 7 for 10 minutes. Turn out sponge on to a sheet of greaseproof paper dusted with caster sugar. Peel off lining paper and trim edges with a sharp knife. Spread with 2 tablespoons honey and roll up at once. When cool, cut off a slice to form 'stump'.

Cream the butter, icing sugar and milk together until smooth. Place the Swiss roll on a plate or board with the 'stump' at the side and cover with butter cream. Melt the chocolate in a small bowl over a saucepan of boiling water. Fill a paper piping bag, fitted with a plain icing nozzle, with the melted chocolate and pipe lines of chocolate on log to resemble the bark of a tree. Finish off the log by dusting around with a little sieved icing sugar and decorate with a sprig of holly.

Christmas Ring Cake

	Imperial	Metric	American
Plain flour	4 oz	100 g	1 cup
Self-raising flour or flour sifted with ½ tsp baking powder	4 oz	100 g	1 cup
Butter	6 oz	150 g	¾ cup
Caster sugar	6 oz	150 g	¾ cup
Vanilla essence	1 tsp	1 tsp	1 tsp
Eggs	3	3	3
Milk	2 tbsp	2 tbsp	2 tbsp
Icing			
Icing sugar	1 lb	450 g	3½ cups
Water	4 tbsp	4 tbsp	4 tbsp
Squeeze of lemon juice			
Decoration			
Almond paste	2 oz	50 g	2 oz
Few drops of red and green colourings			

Grease and lightly flour a 2 pint/1 litre ring tin. Alternately, use a 7 in/17.5 cm round deep cake tin. Sieve the flours together. Cream the butter, sugar and vanilla essence together until light and fluffy. Add the eggs gradually, with a little flour, beating the mixture well. Fold in the remaining flour. Add milk to obtain a dropping consistency. Bake at 350 °F/180 °C/Gas Mark 4 for 1 hour. Sieve icing sugar into a bowl, add the water and lemon juice and beat well. Cover the cake with half the icing, spreading evenly. Place damp greaseproof paper on top of the other half of the icing. When the first coat has dried, cover the cake with the remaining icing. Divide the marzipan into two, colour half green and half red. Shape the green marzipan into holly leaves and the red into berries. Use to decorate the ring cake.

Chapter Five

LITTLE CAKES

It is often nicer to bake a batch of small cakes instead of one large one. This means that perhaps you can offer two or three kinds to guests, and even for the family they will come up looking fresh and exciting on a second day, whereas a cut cake can look tired and crumbly. Some little cakes can be very simple, but they can all be varied with different icings or flavourings – make them in little paper cases for added attraction, or otherwise cook them in deep bun tins. Even rather special cakes such as meringues, brandy snaps and eclairs are not difficult to make if the instructions are followed carefully, and they are useful for parties or even as sweet courses.

Coconut Kisses

	Imperial	Metric	American
Egg whites	*4*	*4*	*4*
Salt	*½ tsp*	*½ tsp*	*½ tsp*
Caster sugar	*10 oz*	*300 g*	*1¼ cups*
Dessicated or shredded			
coconut	*6 oz*	*150 g*	*1½ cups*
Glacé cherries			

Whisk the egg whites and salt until stiff but not dry. Add sugar slowly, beating until dissolved. Fold in the coconut and drop teaspoonfuls on non-stick baking parchment placed on ungreased baking sheets. Bake at 350 °F/180 °C/Gas Mark 4 for 20 minutes. Lift off carefully on to a wire rack to cool, and decorate each with a piece of glacé cherry.

Raisin Bran Buns

	Imperial	Metric	American
Self-raising flour or flour sifted with 1 tsp baking powder	4 oz	100 g	1 cup
Salt	½ tsp	½ tsp	½ tsp
Sugar	2 oz	50 g	¼ cup
Margarine	2 oz	50 g	¼ cup
Raisins	2 oz	50 g	½ cup
All-Bran cereal	2 oz	50 g	½ cup
Egg	1	1	1
Milk	5 tbsp	5 tbsp	5 tbsp

Sieve the flour and salt together and stir in the sugar. Rub in the margarine and then mix in the other ingredients. Put into 12 greased deep bun tins, muffin pans or paper cases. Bake at 400 °F/200 °C/Gas Mark 6 for 15 minutes.

Cup Cakes

	Imperial	Metric	American
Butter or margarine	2 oz	50 g	¼ cup
Caster sugar	2 oz	50 g	¼ cup
Egg	1	1	1
Self-raising flour or flour sifted with ½ tsp baking powder	2 oz	50 g	½ cup
Milk or water to mix			
Flavouring			
Glacé icing			

Cream the fat and sugar until light and fluffy. Add the egg and fold in the sieved flour. Mix with a little milk or water to give a soft dropping consistency and add flavouring. Put into 12 paper cases on a baking sheet. Bake at 375 °F/190 °C/Gas Mark 5 for 10—15 minutes. Ice and decorate when cool.

Bran Spice Cakes

	Imperial	Metric	American
Butter or margarine	3 oz	75 g	⅓ cup
Honey	6 tbsp	6 tbsp	6 tbsp
Egg	1	1	1
Self-raising flour or flour sifted with 2 tsp baking powder	8 oz	225 g	2 cups
Salt	½ tsp	½ tsp	½ tsp
Ground cloves	½ tsp	½ tsp	½ tsp
Ground cinnamon	1 tsp	1 tsp	1 tsp
All-Bran cereal	1½ oz	40 g	½ cup
Raisins	4 oz	100 g	1 cup
Glacé icing			

Cream the fat and honey and beat well together. Add the egg and beat well. Stir in the dry ingredients and the raisins. Put into 18 paper cases on a baking sheet. Bake at 350 °F/180°C/Gas Mark 4 for 20 minutes. Cool and top with a little glacé icing.

Chocolate Orange Buns

	Imperial	Metric	American
Butter or margarine	2 oz	50 g	1/4 cup
Caster sugar	2 oz	50 g	1/4 cup
Egg	1	1	1
Self-raising flour or flour sifted with 1 tsp baking powder	3 oz	75 g	3/4 cup
Orange	1	1	1
Plain chocolate (sweetened)	2 oz	50 g	1/4 cup

Cream the fat and sugar until light and fluffy. Add the egg a little at a time and fold in the sieved flour. Grate the orange rind and squeeze out the juice. Add the orange rind to the cake mixture with enough orange juice to give a soft dropping consistency. Chop the chocolate into small pieces and stir into the mixture. Put into 12 paper cases on a baking sheet. Bake at 375 °F/190 °C/Gas Mark 5 for 10—15 minutes.

Macaroons

	Imperial	Metric	American
Egg whites	2	2	2
Ground almonds	6 oz	150 g	1 1/2 cups
Caster sugar	8 oz	225 g	1 cup
Rice paper			
Blanched almonds			

Whip the egg whites to stiff peaks. Fold in the almonds and sugar and spoon small heaps on to rice paper placed on baking sheets. Put a blanched almond on each. Bake at 350 °F/180 °C/Gas Mark 4 for 20 minutes. Lift on to a wire rack to cook and trim off surplus rice paper.

Orange Butterfly Cakes

	Imperial	Metric	American
Self-raising flour or flour sifted with 1½ tsp baking powder	6 oz	150 g	1½ cups
Salt	¼ tsp	¼ tsp	¼ tsp
Caster sugar	5 oz	125 g	⅔ cup
Orange	1	1	1
Cooking oil	5 tbsp	5 tbsp	5 tbsp
Cold water	5 tbsp	5 tbsp	5 tbsp
Eggs	2	2	2
Icing			
Butter	3 oz	75 g	⅓ cup
Icing sugar	6 oz	150 g	¾ cup
Milk or water	1—2 tbsp	1—2 tbsp	1—2 tbsp

Heat oven to 350 °F/180 °C/Gas Mark 4. Place
flour, salt and sugar in mixing bowl. Add grated
orange rind. Beat together oil, water and egg yolks and
add to dry ingredients. Mix thoroughly. Fold in egg
whites which have been whisked until just stiff. Divide
mixture between 12—14 paper cake cases or greased
bun tins/muffin pans. Bake for 20 minutes until golden
and well-risen. Cool on wire rack. Cream butter until
smooth and gradually beat in icing sugar. Beat in
sufficient milk to give a piping consistency. Cut a slice
from the top of each cake, ¼ in/65 mm from the edge,
then cut each slice in half. Pipe or spread butter icing
in centre of each cake. Replace 'tops' at an angle in
the icing, to represent butterfly wings. Cut pith away
from orange and cut between membranes to release
segments. Decorate top of each cake with an orange
segment.

Eccles Cakes

	Imperial	Metric	American
Puff pastry	6 oz	150 g	6 oz
Currants	2 oz	50 g	½ cup
Chopped mixed peel	1 oz	25 g	¼ cup
Sugar	1 oz	25 g	2 tbsp
Ground allspice	¼ tsp	¼ tsp	¼ tsp
Pinch of ground nutmeg			
Butter	½ oz	15 g	1 tbsp
Egg white	1	1	1
Caster sugar	1 oz	25 g	2 tbsp

Roll out the pastry and cut into large rounds. Mix the currants, peel, sugar, spices and softened butter together. Put 2 teaspoons of the mixture on each pastry circle. Close up the rounds by drawing up the pastry edge, and flatten with a rolling pin. Turn over and place on a baking sheet. Slash the top of each with a sharp knife. Brush over with egg white and sprinkle with caster sugar. Bake at 450 °F/230 °C/Gas Mark 8 for 10 minutes.

Brandy Snaps

	Imperial	Metric	American
Butter	2 oz	50 g	¼ cup
Caster sugar	2 oz	50 g	¼ cup
Black treacle or molasses	2 oz	50 g	2 tbsp
Lemon juice	1 tsp	1 tsp	1 tsp
Plain flour	2 oz	50 g	½ cup
Ground ginger	1 tsp	1 tsp	1 tsp

Melt butter, sugar, black treacle and lemon juice together over a gentle heat. Add sieved flour and ginger and blend together. Put teaspoonfuls of the mixture on well-greased baking trays, 5 in/12.5 cm apart. Bake for 8—10 minutes at 350 °F/180 °C/Gas Mark 4, until a rich brown and well spread. Remove from the oven and leave to cool for a moment until they are easily lifted. While still warm wrap each one around a wooden spoon handle, working quickly. Allow to become firm before lifting on to a wire tray. Store in an airtight tin. Serve plain or filled with fresh cream.

Meringues

	Imperial	Metric	American
Egg whites	2	2	2
Caster sugar	4 oz	100 g	½ cup

Whisk egg whites until they stand in stiff peaks. Fold in sugar and put in tablespoonfuls on baking sheet lined with non-stick baking parchment. Bake at 250 °F/125 °C/Gas Mark ½ for 2 hours. Remove carefully to wire rack to cool. Put together with whipped cream or ice-cream.

Choux Buns

	Imperial	Metric	American
Water	¼ pint	125 ml	⅝ cup
Lard	2 oz	50 g	¼ cup
Plain flour	2¼ oz	58 g	½ cup
Pinch of salt			
Eggs	2	2	2
Double cream			
Icing sugar			

Boil the water and lard. As soon as the mixture boils, put in the flour and salt very quickly and draw off the heat. Beat very hard with a wooden spoon until smooth. Return to heat and cook for 3 minutes, beating very hard. Cool and then beat in the eggs a little at a time until the paste is smooth, glossy and stiff enough to stand in peaks. Do not add all the eggs unless necessary to achieve the right texture. Put in spoonfuls on a greased baking sheet. Bake at 425 °F/220 °C/Gas Mark 7 for 30 minutes. Put on a wire rack to cool. Split and fill with whipped cream and dust with icing sugar.

For **eclairs** pipe into finger lengths and bake. Fill with cream and ice with chocolate or coffee glacé icing.

Chapter Six

BISCUITS AND COOKIES

Many people never think of making their own biscuits, but it is possible to make a large batch of tempting treats for the cost of a single packet of the bought variety. Biscuits may be savoury, to go with cheese, or to use as cocktail snacks, or they may be sweet and simple, or filled and topped excitingly. There are various ways of making biscuits, and some are very quick to prepare. Dough may be rolled out and cut into shapes; or the dough may be baked in a square tin and then cut in squares; or spoonfuls may be placed on baking sheets and pressed flat before baking.

Butter Rusks

	Imperial	Metric	American
Plain flour	8 oz	225 g	2 cups
Baking powder	1½ tsps	1½ tsps	1½ tsps
Pinch of salt			
Butter	3 oz	75 g	⅜ cup
A little milk			

Sift together the flour, baking powder and salt. Rub in the butter and add enough milk to make a fairly soft dough. Roll out 1 in/2.5 cm thick and cut into 2 in/5 cm rounds. Put on a greased baking sheet and bake at 425 °F/220 °C/Gas Mark 7 for 15 minutes. Split each rusk open horizontally with the fingers to give a rough surface and put back on the baking sheet, cut side up. Continue baking for 15 minutes until golden. Cool on a wire rack.

Chocolate Cherry Crunchies

	Imperial	Metric	American
Plain flour	3 oz	75 g	¾ cup
Baking powder	1 tsp	1 tsp	1 tsp
Salt	½ tsp	½ tsp	½ tsp
Glacé cherries	4 oz	100 g	½ cup
Chocolate chips	4 oz	100 g	⅔ cup
Eggs	2	2	2
Sugar	3 oz	75 g	⅓ cup

Sift the flour, baking powder and salt. Add chopped cherries and chocolate chips. Beat together the eggs and sugar in a separate bowl, and fold in the dry mixture. Drop teaspoonfuls on a well-greased baking tray. Bake at 325 °F/170 °C/Gas Mark 3 for 12 minutes. Cool on a wire rack.

Cheesey Pinwheels

	Imperial	Metric	American
Margarine	2 oz	50 g	¼ cup
Self-raising flour or flour sifted with 2 tsp baking powder	8 oz	225 g	2 cups
Generous pinch of salt			
Pinch of cayenne pepper			
Grated Cheddar cheese	1 oz	25 g	4 tbsp
Milk	4 tbsp	4 tbsp	4 tbsp
Egg	1	1	1
Filling			
Tomato purée	3 tbsp	3 tbsp	3 tbsp
Meaux mustard	2 tbsp	2 tbsp	2 tbsp
Onion	1	1	1
Cheddar cheese	1 oz	25 g	4 tbsp

Rub margarine into dry ingredients and stir in cheese. Add milk and egg reserving a little. Mix to form a soft dough and roll out into an oblong, approximately 14 × 7 in/35 × 17.5 cm. Spread with tomato purée, leaving a margin on long side, then spread with mustard. Sprinkle over the finely chopped onion and grated cheese. Brush the margins with the remaining egg mixture and roll up lengthways like a Swiss roll. Cut into 16 pieces and bake at 425 °F/220 °C/Gas Mark 7 for 20 minutes.

Savoury Biscuits

	Imperial	Metric	American
Butter	3 oz	75 g	3/8 cup
Plain flour	8 oz	225 g	2 cups
Good pinch of salt			
Good pinch of pepper			
Mustard powder	1 tsp	1 tsp	1 tsp
Grated Parmesan cheese	1 oz	25 g	1/8 cup
Egg yolk	1	1	1
Water	3—4 tbsp	3—4 tbsp	3—4 tbsp

Sieve the flour, salt, pepper and mustard powder together. Rub the butter into the sieved ingredients until the mixture resembles fine breadcrumbs. Stir in the cheese and add the egg yolk and water. Mix to form a stiff dough and knead lightly with finger tips. Roll out thinly on to a floured working surface and, using different shaped cutters, cut out biscuits. Place biscuits on to a lightly greased baking sheet and prick with a fork. Sprinkle some of the biscuits with poppy seeds, caraway seeds or a little cayenne pepper. Re-roll the pastry trimmings to an oblong 5 in/12.5 cm wide and cut 3 in/7.5 cm strips. Brush the centre of each strip with a little water and sprinkle with chopped almonds or grated Cheddar cheese. Form into twists and place on a lightly greased baking sheet. Bake biscuits for 15—20 minutes at 350 °F/180 °C/Gas Mark 4 until golden brown. Cool on a wire rack.

Chocolate Crumb Cake

	Imperial	Metric	American
Broken sweet biscuits	8 oz	225 g	½ lb
Butter	4 oz	100 g	½ cup
Sugar	1 tbsp	1 tbsp	1 tbsp
Golden syrup	1 tbsp	1 tbsp	1 tbsp
Cocoa	2 tbsp	2 tbsp	2 tbsp
Plain semi-sweet chocolate	4 oz	100 g	4—5 oz

Put the biscuits into a bag and crush them finely with a rolling pin. Cream the butter and sugar and work in the cocoa and syrup. Mix well and blend in the biscuit crumbs until they are coated with the chocolate mixture. Press into a greased foil tray or flan ring about 1 in deep. Chill for 5 hours. Melt the chocolate and pour over the top. Cool and cut in squares to serve. This is a good way of making a rich and filling cake, which can also be eaten after a meal instead of a pudding, and which needs no cooking.

Oat Cakes

	Imperial	Metric	American
Fine oatmeal	6 oz	150 g	1½ cups
Plain flour	2 oz	50 g	½ cup
Salt	½ tsp	½ tsp	½ tsp
Lard or dripping	1 oz	25 g	2 tbsp
Boiling water			

Mix together the oatmeal, flour and salt. Add the melted fat and enough boiling water to make a stiff paste. Roll out very thinly and cut into triangles or rounds. Put on a greased baking sheet and bake at 350 °F/180 °C/Gas Mark 4 for 30 minutes. Lift carefully on a wire rack to cool.

Chocolate Brownies

	Imperial	Metric	American
Sugar	8 oz	225 g	1 cup
Cocoa	1½ oz	40 g	¼ cup
Self-raising flour or flour sifted with ¾ tsp baking powder	3 oz	75 g	¾ cup
Salt	½ tsp	½ tsp	½ tsp
Eggs	2	2	2
Butter or margarine	4 oz	100 g	½ cup
Plain semi-sweet chocolate	4 oz	100 g	4—5 oz

Stir together the sugar, cocoa, flour and salt. Beat eggs and milk and pour into dry mixture. Melt the fat and beat into the mixture. Pour into a greased 8 x 12 in/20 x 30 cm tin and bake at 350 °F/180 °C/Gas Mark 4 for 30 minutes. Cool in the tin and cover with chocolate melted over hot water.

Date Bran Fingers

	Imperial	Metric	American
Eggs	2	2	2
Soft brown sugar	6 oz	150 g	¾ cup
Self-raising flour or flour sifted			
with ¾ tsp baking powder	3 oz	75 g	¾ cup
Pinch of salt			
All-Bran cereal	2 oz	50 g	1 cup
Chopped mixed nuts	2 oz	50 g	½–⅔ cup
Dates	2 oz	50 g	⅓ cup

Whisk the eggs and sugar together until pale and creamy. Sieve in the flour and salt and stir in the cereal, nuts and chopped dates. Put into a greased 7 x 11 in/17.5 x 27.5 cm tin. Bake at 350 °F/180 °C/Gas Mark 4 for 30 minutes. Turn on to a wire rack to cool and cut into fingers.

Sugar Biscuits

	Imperial	Metric	American
Plain flour	4 oz	100 g	1 cup
Rice flour	4 oz	100 g	1 cup
Caster sugar	3 oz	75 g	3/8 cup
Margarine	3 oz	75 g	3/8 cup
Vanilla essence	1/2 tsp	1/2 tsp	1/2 tsp
Egg yolk	1	1	1

Stir together the flour, rice flour and sugar. Rub in the margarine and add the essence. Mix the egg yolk with a very little water and mix into the other ingredients to make a smooth dough. Roll out thinly and cut into shapes. Put on a greased and floured baking sheet and bake at 350 °F/180 °C/Gas Mark 4 for 12 minutes. Sprinkle with a little sugar and lift off carefully. Cool on a wire rack.

Raisin Crisps

	Imperial	Metric	American
Eggs	2	2	2
Seedless raisins	6 oz	150 g	1 cup
Vanilla essence	1 tsp	1 tsp	1 tsp
Salt	1 tsp	1 tsp	1 tsp
Salad oil	1/4 pint	125 ml	2/3 cup
Soft brown sugar	8 oz	225 g	1 cup
Oatmeal	12 oz	350 g	2 cups
Desiccated coconut	3 oz	75 g	1 cup

Beat the eggs lightly and stir in the remaining ingredients. Drop spoonfuls on to greased baking sheets and press with the back of a spoon into 2 in/5 cm rounds. Bake at 350 °F/180 °C/Gas Mark 4 for 10 minutes until golden brown. Cool on wire rack.

Sandwich Biscuits

	Imperial	Metric	American
Plain flour	3 oz	75 g	¾ cup
Cornflour	1 oz	25 g	3 tbsp
Butter	3 oz	75 g	⅜ cup
Sugar	2 oz	50 g	¼ cup
Instant coffee powder	2 tsps	2 tsps	2 tsps
Water	1 tbsp	1 tbsp	1 tbsp
Butter icing			
Glacé icing			

Sieve together the flour and cornflour. Cream the butter and sugar until light and fluffy. Mix coffee and water and stir into the creamed mixture. Add the flour and knead to a smooth dough. Roll out thinly and cut into circles with a scone cutter. Put on a greased baking sheet and bake at 350 °F/180 °C/Gas Mark 4 for 10 minutes. Cool on a wire rack. Put together in pairs with butter icing and finish the tops with glacé icing. Either match the flavours of icing, such as orange butter icing and orange glacé icing *or* contrast the filling with the topping. Try a coffee or vanilla filling and chocolate topping for instance.

Bourbon Biscuits

	Imperial	Metric	American
Plain flour	3 oz	75 g	¾ cup
Cocoa	½ oz	15 g	1½ tbsp
Margarine	2 oz	50 g	¼ cup
Caster sugar	2 oz	50 g	¼ cup
Egg yolk	1	1	1
Vanilla essence	¼ tsp	¼ tsp	¼ tsp
A little water			
Plain semi-sweet chocolate	3 oz	75 g	3—4 oz

Sieve together the flour and cocoa. Cream the fat and sugar and work in the egg yolk, essence, flour mixture and a little water to make a stiff dough. Roll out thinly and cut into rectangles about 3 x 1 in/7.5 x 2.5 cm. Put on a greased baking sheet and bake at 350 °F/180 °C/Gas Mark 4 for 10 minutes. Cool on a wire rack. Put together pairs of biscuits with a little melted chocolate and dust the tops with a little extra sugar.

Ginger Nuts

	Imperial	Metric	American
Plain flour	6 oz	150 g	1½ cups
Pinch of salt			
Ground ginger	2 tsps	2 tsps	2 tsps
Ground cinnamon	½ tsp	½ tsp	½ tsp
Ground mixed spice	½ tsp	½ tsp	½ tsp
Butter	2 oz	50 g	¼ cup
Soft brown sugar	4 oz	100 g	½ cup
Golden syrup	1 tbsp	1 tbsp	1 tbsp

Sieve the flour, salt and spices together. Cream the butter and sugar and work in the golden syrup and the dry ingredients to make a stiff paste. Roll out and cut into small rounds with a scone cutter. Put on a greased baking sheet and bake at 325 °F/170 °C/Gas Mark 3 for 15 minutes. Lift off carefully and cool on a wire rack.

Sticky Flapjacks

	Imperial	Metric	American
Butter	3 oz	75 g	⅜ cup
Demerara sugar	3 oz	75 g	⅜ cup
Clear honey	6 tbsp	6 tbsp	6 tbsp
Porridge oats	5 oz	125 g	1⅔ cups

Put butter, sugar and clear honey into a saucepan and heat gently until butter has melted. Remove from heat, add oats and mix well together. Spread mixture over the base of a greased 7 x 11 in/17.5 x 27.5 cm oblong tin. Bake at 350 °F/180 °C/Gas Mark 4 for about 20 minutes. Mark into fingers while still warm. When cold cut fingers apart and remove from tin with a broad-bladed knife.

Scotch Shortbread

	Imperial	Metric	American
Plain flour	7 oz	175 g	1¾ cups
Rice flour	1 oz	25 g	4 tbsp
Salt	¼ tsp	¼ tsp	½ tsp
Butter	4 oz	100 g	½ cup
Caster sugar	2 oz	50 g	¼ cup

Sieve together the flour, rice flour and salt. Rub the butter into the dry ingredients until the mixture is like fine crumbs, and stir in the sugar. Knead well to a pliable paste. Roll out on a well-floured board into a circle. Crimp the edges, mark into wedges and prick all over with a fork. Put on a greased baking sheet. Bake at 325 °F/170 °C/Gas Mark 3 for 35 minutes until pale golden brown. Lift off carefully and cool on a wire rack. Dust with sugar when cold.

Crunchies

	Imperial	Metric	American
Lard	2 oz	50 g	¼ cup
Margarine	2 oz	50 g	¼ cup
Sugar	3 oz	75 g	⅜ cup
Golden syrup	1 tsp	1 tsp	1 tsp
Boiling water	3 tsps	3 tsps	3 tsps
Vanilla essence	½ tsp	½ tsp	½ tsp
Self-raising flour or flour sifted with 1 tsp baking powder	4 oz	100 g	1 cup
Porridge oats	2 oz	50 g	⅔ cup

Cream together the fats and sugar. Stir in the syrup, water and essence. Add the flour and oats and mix very thoroughly. Roll into 30 balls and put on a greased baking sheet. Bake at 350 °F/180 °C/Gas Mark 4 for 15 minutes. Cool on a wire rack.

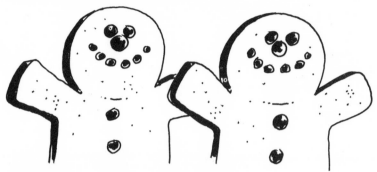

Gingerbread Men

	Imperial	Metric	American
Plain flour	9 oz	250 g	2⅛ cups
Ground ginger	2 tsps	2 tsps	2 tsps
Ground cinnamon	½ tsp	½ tsp	½ tsp
Ground mixed spice	½ tsp	½ tsp	½ tsp
Margarine	4 oz	100 g	½ cup
Clear honey	4 tbsp	4 tbsp	4 tbsp

Sieve the flour and spices into a bowl and rub the margarine into the flour. Add the honey and mix into the flour to form a soft, not sticky dough. Knead lightly on a well-floured surface and roll out to about ¼ in/65 mm thick. Cut out the shapes required and place on greased baking trays. Bake at 350°F/180 °C/Gas Mark 4 for about 15 minutes until light brown. Leave to cool on the baking sheets.

These gingerbread men can either be decorated before baking with pieces of glacé cherries for the mouth and currants representing the eyes or they can be decorated when cold with icing.

Ginger Shortie

	Imperial	Metric	American
Self-raising flour	6 oz	150 g	1½ cups
Ground ginger	4 tsps	4 tsps	4 tsps
Butter	4 oz	100 g	½ cup
Caster sugar	3 oz	75 g	⅜ cup
Egg	1	1	1
Ginger marmalade	2 tbsp	2 tbsp	2 tbsp
Sifted icing sugar	4 oz	100 g	⅔ cup
Crystallised ginger			

Sieve the flour with the ginger and rub in the butter. Add sugar and enough beaten egg to bind the mixture together. Turn on to a lightly floured surface, divide mixture in half and knead lightly. Roll into two 7 in/17.5 cm circles to fit the tin. Place one circle in the tin, spread over the ginger marmalade, then lift the other circle on top. Bake at 350 °F/180 °C/Gas Mark 4 for about 50 minutes until golden brown. Turn the shortcake on to a wire tray to cool. Mix the icing sugar with just enough water or orange juice to make a smooth glacé icing; spread over the top of the shortcake. Decorate with pieces of crystallised ginger.

Chocolate Raisin Drops

	Imperial	Metric	American
Butter or margarine	8 oz	225 g	1 cup
Brown sugar	8 oz	225 g	1 cup
Plain chocolate	2 oz	50 g	2 oz
Eggs	3	3	3
Milk	1/4 pint	125 ml	5/8 cup
Vanilla essence	1 tsp	1 tsp	1 tsp
Plain flour	8 oz	225 g	2 cups
Salt	1 tsp	1 tsp	1 tsp
Baking powder	2 tsps	2 tsps	2 tsps
Bicarbonate of soda	1/2 tsp	1/2 tsp	1/2 tsp
Seedless raisins	8 oz	225 g	1 1/3 cups
Melted chocolate			

Cream butter and sugar together thoroughly.
Melt chocolate in bowl over saucepan of hot water.
Allow to cool and add to creamed mixture. Stir in
beaten eggs and milk and vanilla essence. Sieve flour,
salt, baking powder and bicarbonate of soda, and fold
into creamed mixture. Stir in raisins. Drop
tablespoonfuls of the mixture on to a greased baking
sheet. Bake at 375 °F/190 °C/Gas Mark 5 for 10—12
minutes. Top each raisin drop with melted chocolate.

Honolulu Cookies

	Imperial	Metric	American
Plain flour	8 oz	225 g	2 cups
Baking powder	1 tsp	1 tsp	1 tsp
Salt	½ tsp	½ tsp	½ tsp
Lard	1½ oz	40 g	3 tbsp
Smooth peanut butter	6 tbsp	6 tbsp	6 tbsp
Caster sugar	6 oz	150 g	¾ cup
Egg	1	1	1
Can pineapple (drained)	1 lb	450 g	1½ cups
Glacé cherries			

Sieve flour, baking powder and salt into a mixing bowl. Cream lard, peanut butter and sugar together until light and fluffy. Add egg gradually, beating well. Cut pineapple into small pieces and add to creamed mixture. Mix well. Place heaped teaspoonfuls of mixture on a greased baking tray. Put a piece of glacé cherry on top of each. Bake at 375°F/190 °C/Gas Mark 5 for 20 minutes.

Honey Lemon Dreams

	Imperial	Metric	American
Butter or margarine	4 oz	100 g	½ cup
Caster sugar	4 oz	100 g	½ cup
Egg	1	1	1
Clear honey	4 tbsp	4 tbsp	4 tbsp
Plain flour	9 oz	250 g	2¼ cups
Baking powder	1 tsp	1 tsp	1 tsp
Salt			
Chopped mixed peel			
Lemon curd			

Cream the butter and sugar together until light

and fluffy. Beat egg and honey together and add to the
creamed mixture. Sieve the flour, baking powder and
salt together and fold into the mixture. Put
teaspoonfuls of mixture on greased baking sheets.
Flatten the tops with a dampened fork and put a little
peel on top. Bake at 350 °F/180 °C/Gas Mark 4 for
15—20 minutes. Cool slightly, remove from baking
sheets, cool and sandwich together with a little lemon
curd.

Cherry Chocolate Chip Cookies

	Imperial	Metric	American
Butter	4 oz	100 g	½ cup
Soft brown sugar	4 oz	100 g	½ cup
Egg	1	1	1
Clear honey	1 tbsp	1 tbsp	1 tbsp
Self-raising flour or flour sifted with 2 tsp baking powder	8 oz	225 g	2 cups
Chopped glacé cherries	2 oz	50 g	½ cup
Chocolate, semi-sweet or chips	2 oz	50 g	2 oz

Cream butter and sugar together until light and
fluffy. Gradually beat in the egg and lastly the honey.
Stir in the flour to make a soft paste. Divide in half.
Add the chopped cherries to one half and the chopped
chocolate to the other half. Grease and flour two
baking trays. Set oven at 350 °F/180 °C/Gas Mark 4.
Using a teaspoon, place rounded mounds of the
mixture on baking tray leaving plenty of space around
each mound. Using wet fingers press the mounds down
on to the baking sheets. Bake for about 10—12
minutes. Leave to cool on tray before removing to
cooling rack.

Waffles

	Imperial	Metric	American
Plain flour	6 oz	150 g	¾ cup
Pinch of salt			
Baking powder	3 tsps	3 tsps	3 tsps
Caster sugar	1 oz	25 g	2 tbsp
Eggs	2	2	2
Milk	½ pint	250 ml	1¼ cups
Butter	2 oz	50 g	¼ cup

Melted butter to grease waffle pan

Sift the flour, salt and baking powder into a bowl and stir in the sugar. Make a well in the centre and drop in the egg yolks. Mix with a wooden spoon, gradually adding milk and melted butter alternately. Whisk egg whites until stiff but not dry and fold into the batter with a metal spoon. Grease and heat waffle iron and brush with a little melted butter. Spoon some of the batter into the waffle iron and cook for 1—2 minutes on each side until golden brown. Serve the waffles hot with clear honey or syrup. A frying pan can be used instead of a waffle iron. Grease the pan lightly and drop in a tablespoon of the mixture. Cook on each side until golden brown.

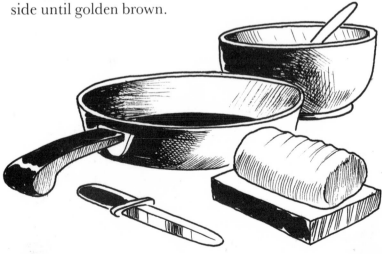

Chapter Seven

ICINGS

Many cakes need no filling or topping, while others are perfectly satisfactory with a filling of jam or whipped cream, or a topping of sifted icing sugar or of caster sugar. When something more elaborate is needed, make up a simple butter icing for a filling and/or topping, or combine it with a glacé icing for a topping. For fruit cakes for special occasions, almond paste and royal icing are traditional toppings.

Basic Butter Icing

	Imperial	Metric	American
Butter	4 oz	100 g	½ cup
Icing sugar	8 oz	225 g	1¾ cup
Milk, fruit juice or hot water	2 tbsp	2 tbsp	2 tbsp
Flavouring			

Cream the butter until soft and gradually beat in the sugar, liquid and flavouring until the icing is soft and creamy. Flavour icing with coffee or other essence, with grated fruit peel and juice or with cocoa.

Glacé Icing

	Imperial	Metric	American
Icing sugar	4 oz	100 g	2/3 cup
Warm water	2 tbsp	2 tbsp	2 tbsp
Flavouring			

Put the sugar, water and flavouring into a small thick pan and heat until just warm, stirring to dissolve the sugar. The icing will look smooth and glossy. Glacé icing should coat the back of a spoon quite thickly and not be runny.

Almond Paste

	Imperial	Metric	American
Icing sugar	4 oz	100 g	2/3 cup
Caster sugar	4 oz	100 g	1/2 cup
Ground almonds	8 oz	225 g	2 cups
Lemon juice	1 tsp	1 tsp	1 tsp
Few drops of almond essence			
Beaten egg to mix			

Stir the sugars together. Add the ground almonds, lemon juice and almond essence, with enough egg to bind the mixture and give a firm dough. Knead lightly on a sugared board. Cakes should be brushed with a little sieved raspberry or apricot jam, or redcurrant jelly, before the almond paste is put on top.

Royal Icing

	Imperial	Metric	American
Egg whites	4	4	4
Icing sugar	2 lb	1 kg	7 cups
Lemon juice	1 tbsp	1 tbsp	1 tbsp
Glycerine	2 tsps	2 tsps	2 tsps

Whisk the egg whites until slightly frothy and stir in the sugar gradually. When half the sugar has been mixed in, add the lemon juice. Add the remaining sugar, beating well until the mixture forms soft peaks when pulled up with a spoon. Stir in the glycerine and put icing in a covered bowl for 24 hours before use. Beat lightly before using. For piping, it may be necessary to add a little more sugar to give the correct stiffness.

INDEX